# Garden Stories

# Garden Stories

JUDY RICHTER

ISBN: 1542932491
ISBN 13: 9781542932493

*For Aleida and Cici*

# Contents

# Acknowledgments

Special thanks for the thoughtful and artful illustrations provided by former director of the University of Northern Colorado School of Nursing, now accomplished artist and dear friend, Sandy Baird.

Thanks to the many gardeners in our community who shared their garden stories for the benefit of the Greeley Garden Tour. Each of the garden stories influenced my gardening and my writing.

The Greeley Garden Tour committee were partners and friends in hosting the annual tour. Special thanks to Leona Kepler, who has been a member of the committee since its inception more than twenty years ago; to Ruth Quade, Water Conservation Coordinator, city of Greeley Water Department, which champions the importance of xeric gardening; and Jan Martin, a steadfast supporter of the annual tour and the completion of this book.

I learned invaluable information in the certified gardener program offered by the Colorado State University extension program. I am especially appreciative for Jamie Weiss, habitat outreach coordinator for the Audubon Rockies and director of the Wildscape Ambassador program. She instills the importance of planting with natives throughout the northern Colorado region.

My family were steadfast in their encouragement. My sisters, Catherine McEver and Susan Padover, were enthusiastic throughout and enabled me to believe that I had something to offer as a writer.

Once I announced I was writing a book, Dave advised me to write fifteen minutes a day, Juli asked for regular updates on my progress, and Denise pulled me to the finish line by inviting me to attend a writer retreat with her. I smile when I hear their garden stories and delight when I see Aleida and Cici dabbling in the soil. Finally, thanks to Walt, who provided inspiration, hard labor, and support for all our gardening endeavors.

# One

### THE BEGINNING

*Life begins the day you start a garden.*

—*CHINESE PROVERB*

*I* am cradled in a safe, dark, warm room. Waiting. I am waiting for a long while, but I am not afraid. Instead, I am curious about what is ahead. There is movement all around me, but I stay in one place. Then one day, everything changes so that my life before bears no resemblance to what comes after. I feel a cool liquid seep around me. The walls in my room are swelling and cracking, and I am shifting, stretching, *reaching. All of a sudden, I feel a rush, and I am floating. After some gentle bumps and lifts, I land on a soft space where it is light and warm. Soft, moist fingers around me crumble a bit in a quick burst of rain, and I am once again safe under a soft blanket of earth. After a short rest, I am ready to move. I stretch to each side and wiggle below, pushing and sliding through the soft floor. I reach above to the light and feel the cool air illuminated by the intense sunlight. I am awake now. I can begin.*

When *does* the garden story begin? Does it begin with the first pop of a seedling into a tiny green shoot? Or is it when I enter the garden and notice that little green shoot? I think there are as many stories in the garden as there are characters in the ever-changing drama. I think of myself as just one member of the garden community. All members have their own entrances and roles to play on the lively interactive stage.

I believe my story began when I decided to take the leap from dabbling in the perennial bed to developing a real relationship with the garden. The garden is alive with the possibility of transformation in juxtaposition with character defects.

Gardens, after all, are a lot like their caretakers, a mixture of treasured features and sections that the gardener would rather not claim as his or her own.

My role as gardener has changed over the years. I started with the naive notion that I could tame the soil and be the master of my garden plot. After numerous failures, I became humble. I realized that my controlling behaviors needed taming. Thankfully, I became more awake from my years of gardening and open to learning lessons from the garden experience. There is no assurance that the garden story will be filled with happily ever after. All stories have conflict, and the garden story is no exception.

My fascination with gardening started when I was a child. I found adventure in the lush green woods behind my grandparents' home, and I was thrilled when my grandfather asked me to help him transplant trees from these woods to a space in his yard. The smells of the Northeast woodland floor comingling with the fragrance of the apple trees in his backyard evokes memories of precious time with my grandfather in the Jersey woods he dearly loved. He didn't have to tell me to care for the earth. I learned that lesson by watching him and working side by side in caring for the trees and shrubs on his property.

During the years of what I refer to as my cluttered life, I struggled with priorities in my academic life as a nursing professor, while trying to be a good wife and mother. The garden was a distraction, but more often than not, it was an annoyance. It represented one more set of looming demands complicated by a burgeoning crop of weeds.

One winter afternoon, when my gloomy mood matched the dark, short days, I went outside to get some light and immediately felt the benefits of pausing to take in the cold, brisk air and the details of the landscape around me. I started to develop a relationship with my garden and became a student of the living world around me. I realized that the garden in winter was spectacular. When I took the time to breathe and open my senses to the seasonal gifts in the garden, my cluttered life became more manageable. The garden became a place of solace.

Whether I am pulling weeds, planting seeds, or moving perennials from one spot to another, I am soothed and refreshed by the sensation of plunging my hands into the soil. Once I connected to the garden, I enjoyed my time there, but I was rather aimless in most of my early adult gardening endeavors. I tucked in garden time as I would a hobby, such as reading. I wasn't a good partner with my garden. Other life commitments would rise to the top of my to-do list, and I would neglect the plants that brought so much joy in their youthful days of radiant bloom. It wasn't until recently, when I launched my third phase of starting over in my garden, that it occurred to me that my garden has a story to tell. If I pay attention, I can hear that story.

Ten years ago, when I retired from my career as a professor of nursing, I became an active volunteer for the annual Greeley Garden Tour. At the same time, I was starting over in my own garden. I knew I had a lot to learn. I plunged into my new volunteer experience by agreeing to write descriptions of each of the six gardens that would be on the tour. This would be a refreshing change from the writing I did during my academic career. Little did I know that the opportunity to visit a diversity of gardens and listen to scores of garden descriptions would not only influence how I garden but also affect me personally. As I listened to garden descriptions, it became apparent that the gardener views the garden as an extension of self.

At first, I was intrigued by the myriad specimens in each garden and the diversity of the shrubs and trees. I was so fascinated with learning all I could about the species I was describing that I didn't focus on the design in front of me. Eventually, I started to see the garden as an entity that was more than the conglomeration of trees, plants, and shrubs that were planted to create a landscape. I began to see stories in each of the gardens. I discovered that each garden is a reflection of the gardener who tends the living world in his or her surroundings.

Dazzling perennials, lush green shrubs, and trees that provide comfort and shade—nice images, but they are just descriptors until they are woven into a story facilitated by a gardener. Now, when I am working in my garden in the first sweet days of spring or walking through my garden in the still silence of winter, I know that there is a story that my garden tells. Some of the characters in my garden story are the plants, trees, and shrubs I have selected to create a theme that is appealing to visiting people and wildlife. The setting for my story was once a prairie with clay soil, little rain, and hot summer temperatures. Snow can make an appearance in the early autumn, winters can be arctic or quite mild, and the spring season is often windy. Late-spring snowstorms often make surprise appearances once the fruit trees are in full bloom. So, the story created by seasonal changes is dynamic and exciting for me as a gardener. I am always learning new lessons about which plants thrive in the ever-changing Colorado weather patterns.

There are also decisions that need to be made about encouraging or eliminating the volunteer plants and wildlife that enter the scene. Are they characters I want to encourage, or do I sweep them from the stage? My relationship with my garden has evolved over time. I have come to the realization that my garden is a reflection of me. The garden has taught me to be patient, to observe, and to listen.

The garden story is a production that sometimes behaves as a play without a director. I recall returning from vacation many times to witness a hostile takeover by the weeds from our surrounding fields. I naturally assume the role of director of the story but depend heavily on feedback from the cast of characters. As director of the story, I make decisions that have an impact on the conflict created by the weeds, pests, and plants that dominate the stage. My garden has undergone transitions and transformations and is a portrait of my values, sprinkled with elements of joy.

My garden story challenges me to enter my garden with an open mind and a willingness to tap into all my senses. Something mysterious and satisfying happens when, as a gardener, I allow my garden to take a leadership role in guiding the story. I recognize the species that thrive in my garden, and I encourage them to expand their parts in the garden story. In my gardening journey, lessons emerged along the way that influenced the way that I garden and also the way that I live. It is apparent to me now that, just as all living things are connected, I am connected to my garden. I am rejuvenated by the seasonal cycle of birth, growth, death, and renewal.

As I mature as a gardener, I pay attention to cues from my garden. Now, for example, I encourage my garden to be in harmony with the surrounding High Plains grasses and wildlife.

The word *garden* conjures up an abundance of images. I picture a lush green park shaded by layers of cool, green shrubs and towering trees or maybe a rolling stretch of spectacular color spilling from the varied blooms of perennials, bulbs, and annuals. Perhaps it is a quiet area for reflection by a rippling waterfall, with orange-speckled fish darting beneath in a pond embracing water lilies that slide ever so gently across the surface. But it can also be a vibrant showcase of cactus species tucked between sandstone rock, massive boulders, or gnarled wood stumps artistically placed in a bed of perennials. Or maybe the garden is an oasis for the gardener who tends hybrid, antique, or vintage roses, each planted in honor of a loved member of the family.

Each of us has a different idea about what the garden holds and how it can serve the needs of his or her unique life. In its most basic form, a garden is a patch of land that is waiting to be transformed to reflect the personality of the gardener. Of course, many of us are so busy with work and family responsibilities that we don't realize the potential lying dormant in our backyard garden, yet to be developed as a wellspring of renewal. Those of us fortunate enough to own a home may also have a yard or plot of grass maintained for family barbecues, a play area for the kids, and a space for the dog to romp.

People turn to gardening for a variety of reasons. But most gardeners find their passion embedded in their roots. I recall visiting one garden that had a spectacular variety of roses. The gardener became a little misty when she said she had moved the shrubs from the homes of her mother and mother-in-law. My friend Kathleen would hold a family competition to see who could grow the biggest pumpkin, a family tradition that endured for years.

I have known some gardeners who raise stunning gladioli and others who have won prizes for their dahlias. I am an appreciative audience for those gardens, but my thumb is not so green as to produce show-stopping flowers.

Some folks focus on vegetable gardening and are committed to sustainability. I have been intrigued by a recent trend of integrating vegetables among the flowers. I tried that myself a few years ago, with pretty good results. There was the hassle, though, of removing the gangly tomato vine from the flower garden bed. I thoroughly enjoyed some aspects of vegetable gardening when our kids were young, but since I am now the only one at home who eats vegetables, I go to the farmers' market.

My husband, Walt, and I had our first experience in gardening when we were newly married, starting our lives together in Vermont. We lived in a housing complex for married students in Winooski, Vermont, while Walt attended graduate school at the University of Vermont. The opportunity to manage a little ten-by-ten plot became available for all residents, and we eagerly signed up. This was my first encounter with community gardening. Those were the "granola days" of the early 1970s when I wore braids and Birks while proudly watering and weeding our little garden. As I look back, it was a gentle and affirming introduction to gardening.

After moving from Vermont to Alabama, Walt and I bought our first home in a suburb of Birmingham. The yard was a tiny, tidy space that needed little upkeep. Walt and I were busy with work and graduate school and had little time for the yard. I couldn't tell you the names of the trees or shrubs that surrounded the house. We didn't do any more maintenance than mowing and pulling enough weeds to feel like respectable neighbors.

When we moved to Colorado and bought a home with a small yard, my interest in gardening was rekindled. Remembering the fun of planting a vegetable garden in Vermont, I was ready to dedicate a section of our backyard to vegetable gardening. Walt rototilled a ten-by-fifteen-foot space behind the house that was in the direct sun, and we tilled some compost into the soil. Since that time, I have learned that it is much healthier for the garden when the soil is hand turned so that worms survive to perform their magic underground. But this is the way we grew vegetables in the late 1970s. We tried our hand at corn, cucumbers, zucchini, tomatoes, green beans, and peppers. Just a toddler, our son, Dave, enjoyed poking seeds into the soil and helping pick ripe produce.

In addition to the vegetable garden, we had four plum trees in the backyard that, for a short while, yielded an abundance of plums. I had a blast making plum sauce for oriental food for a year or two before the plums abruptly refused to bear fruit. At the time, I didn't have a clue about possible causes for the stop in production. Like so many young adults, I didn't have the time for or interest in finding a solution to the plum problem. Instead, I focused on what was working: my burgeoning crop of vegetables.

The story would have continued along for years. Instead, after five years, we made the decision to move to an undeveloped piece of property in west Greeley, where we would build our own home. Today when I tend my gardens, I feel satisfaction and joy watching birds skitter for shelter under the rabbit brush (*Chrysothamnus*) and native nine bark (*Physocarpus opulifolius*). We have lived in our current home for more than thirty years. Where once I took no notice of the garden in winter, now in late November, I find beauty in the naked garden. But I am getting ahead of myself. My garden story, like most stories, has had lots of twists and turns and, of course, some conflict along the way.

# Two

## Garden Stories

*Art is not what you see but
what you make others see.*

*—Degas*

After observing and talking with many gardeners as they show off their gardens, it occurs to me that there are an awful lot of similarities between garden and gardener. Like a family dog that takes on the appearance of her owner, the garden takes on the personality of the gardener. I am growing used to the idea that what I put forward in the garden is an extension of my values and my passion, so of course my garden is a reflection of me. I would have been appalled at that comparison when I was in the depths of my career and my garden looked like hell. But thankfully, my garden and I both continue to evolve.

For the past ten years, I have had the happy job of writing descriptions for each garden on the Greeley Garden Tour. The garden descriptions are embedded in a little booklet, which is also the ticket for admission to the gardens. In the early years of describing the gardens, I focused on the unique features of each garden. I was intrigued by learning about the species that thrived in Colorado, as well as the design of the gardens.

I have observed that gardens offer a banquet for the senses and provide a burst of inspiration for seasoned gardeners, as well as would-be dabblers in the soil. But perhaps most important, I have discovered that the garden tells a story.

All the gardens on the tour are selected because a person is passionate about his or her garden and is ready to share that garden with others. When someone from the community wants to share the beauty and interest of his or her garden, we are grateful to have him or her on our local garden tour. It's just that simple. Word of mouth produces friends of friends who know someone who would like to share his or her garden, and that is how we build our tour. Sounds risky, but it works. A well-meaning perfectionist once asked, "What if someone with an ugly garden steps up and says they want to be on the tour?" I refrained from laughing, but it wasn't hard for me to answer. My firm belief is that if a person thinks he or she has a garden that others will enjoy, then that person is ready to be on our garden tour. I have observed over and over that a garden loved by its caretaker reflects that love in the form of its own unique story. The multitude of ways that an untamed plot of land can be transformed continues to amaze me.

The garden is a microcosm of the gardener's world, or perhaps how he or she wants the world to be. The gardener creates a living space outside of the home that says to the visitor, "This is what I value; this is what brings me joy." For those who are ready to embrace the opportunity to mingle with nature, the yard is ready for transformation into a garden that delights the gardener and visitors.

Entering a garden provides an introduction to the story the gardener wants to share. I was a bit surprised to discover that the story is not revealed with the same information found in an autobiography. For example, I have noticed that one's choice of life work may have little in common with the garden he or she creates. Gardens are more often the mirror of the authentic lives we all strive for. The garden is a living piece of art created by a gardener who may profess to have no artistic talents. Dormant within each of us is a garden ready to be designed and planted. I have discovered a few characteristics in common with the gardeners who are sharing a story in their gardens.

There is a willingness to pause, to observe, and to understand the vibrant personality of the garden. Often, the gardener will describe the land before he or she enters the scene. Some keep a photo journal of the transformation that occurred once a plan was established and a design was created. When gardeners tell their stories, there is intention to partner with their gardens. Most gardeners, when asked, will describe the features of the gardens that they wanted to enhance or highlight. The values, beliefs, and passions of the gardener become embedded in the living artistry that is created. The placement of artifacts and selection of shrubs and perennials provide pieces of the story.

On our garden tour, we feature large estate gardens, small cottage gardens, and gardens in between. There are gardens with an abundance of perennials and expansive vegetable gardens. Sometimes, fine specimens of trees that thrive in our ecosystem are the main characters in the garden story. Some gardens are ancient, and some are brand new. The one thing the gardens have in common is that each is the product of a woman or man with dirt under his or her nails and a knowing smile that reveals pride in his or her garden story.

When I enter each garden, it is somewhat like entering a new culture. I want the gardener to tell me his or her garden story. One of the first questions that I ask each gardener is, "What do you like the best about your garden?" Most initially have a blank stare. The gardener is so intimately intertwined with the garden that it's hard to come up with one answer. In fact, many gardeners have difficulty identifying the plants in their gardens. Sometimes, the gardeners know the common names of plants and trees, but often, they are not sure. They rarely name the genus and species of the vegetation in their yard.

The more I grow in my role as a gardener, the more I want to learn as much as I can about the plants that are my companions. For starters, the proper name of a plant, just like the full name of a person, is an important identifier. The use of common plant names can be confusing. For example, the rose (*Rosa*) family includes more than one hundred species. I would have a lot of trouble finding someone in my town named John if that were the only information I had. I would need to know John's last name. The same is true for finding plants from a nursery. The genus refers to a group of related plants, much like the name *Smith* identifies the family that John belongs to. John is a member of the family, and in plant terms, he is his own unique species. When I look at a plant tag, the genus is always listed first, followed by the species. Knowing the genus and species of a plant allows me to select exactly what I want for my garden. We are fortunate that master gardeners are available the day of our Greeley Garden Tour to help identify the genus and species of plants for the curious visitors.

After pondering the names of the plants on their property, the gardeners dig deeper and find some pithy reasons for their love affairs with their gardens. Responses reflect a potpourri of riches that are found in the gardens. Fences and trellises are adorned with silver lace vine (*Polygonum aubertii*), trumpet vine (*Campsis radicans*), Kintzley's ghost (*Lonicera reticulata*), grapes (*Vitis labrusca*), or English ivy (*Hedera helix*). Gates, doors, windows, iron bed frames, even a toilet seat and bedpan encircle colorful annuals and perennials. Dry creek beds and water features that rumble, ripple, bubble, and form waterfalls swirl into small ponds, and big trickle-down rocks recycle into watering cans and old washtubs. Art that is expensive, handcrafted, nostalgic, or a relic from a family homestead and whimsical crafts created or personally selected by the gardener capture a special memory. Pots—big and little, unique, colorful, antique, rustic—are filled with annuals that pop with color. There are handcrafted play sets, gazebos, decks, hand-tooled picket fences, and raised-garden boxes.

Often, it is the structural aspects of the garden that come to mind first. But is it the artifacts that make the gardens special? They certainly add flair and sometimes whimsy. But there is so much more to the story. I think the magic comes from the interaction of the living and nonliving characters on the stage.

What are the elements of the story? The garden mirrors the personality of the gardener, and it sometimes weaves early childhood memories into the story. It is not uncommon for the gardener to draw inspiration from the childhood home, the gardener's roots. Many gardeners find comfort in tapping into their roots as they select plantings reminiscent of their early years or of loved ones who were an important part of their lives.

One gardener planted a Chinese money plant (*Pilea peperomioides*) at the front of the home. The plant had a heritage that dated back sixty years. The seeds of this exotic perennial traveled with the family to many parts of the country from their original home in Baltimore, Maryland.

My friend Kathleen agreed to have her garden on the tour a few years ago. One of the unique features of her backyard is a protected vegetable garden that is also a habitat for chickens. This functional approach to gardening is reminiscent of her roots. She grew up on the eastern plains of Colorado where her family raised chickens. A deluxe chicken coop provides a home for Darlene, Marlene, Charlene, and Esther. The free-range chickens add bugs to their diet as they groom the leaves of tomatoes and zucchini. The vegetables thrive with attention from "the girls."

Many gardeners are deliberate about creating a memory garden to honor family members or deceased pets. I recall one gardener who had a large cottonwood tree stump carved with the likeness of a recently deceased family dog. Another poignant memory comes to mind of a family who created a special section in their garden to honor their young daughter who had died in a car accident. The family found comfort in the tranquil garden space that reminded them of her. I can sense the peace and gratitude embedded in the transplanted shrub or perennial that once thrived in the garden of a beloved family member. One gardener created a memory garden with roses (*Rosas*) from her mother's garden and peonies (*Paeonia suffruticosa*) from the garden of her mother-in-law.

Gardens tell stories of diversity with the carefully thought-out design and selection of species that reflect the personality of the gardener. The shrubs, trees, and grasses engage in movement even when the air is still—a reminder that the garden is always breathing. One of the gardeners on our tour this year is also an interior designer. He studies each section of his garden from a variety of angles to create the desired effect for the visitor. He advocates movement and artful flow throughout the garden, but he made an unusual decision in one section of his garden. He decided to leave a dead tree standing because it was quite beautiful in the structural form and because it articulated with the lines of living trees in the adjacent space. Naturalists would actually applaud this decision, because dead trees, or snags, serve as nesting space for a variety of birds and insects.

Part of the garden story reveals the experience of the gardener while mingling with the trees; shrubs; flowers; and yes, weeds, bugs, and other pests. What does the gardener do out there? Smell the roses? Well, yes. Gardeners comment on the fragrance of herb gardens, the sweet smell of thyme used as a steppable integrated in garden paths, lavender, peonies, and roses. A number of gardeners comment on their love of wildlife and birds in particular.

Some gardeners incorporate vegetable-and-herb gardens, occasionally integrated with flower beds. I know gardeners who drape their arbors with grapes for wine making and for the table. A few gardeners have even had hops growing over arbors to supplement their beer-brewing hobby. One garden I visited had an entirely edible yard. There was not one perennial, tree, or shrub that lacked the ability to feed the gardener and his family. Even the grass on the lawn, rye, could be harvested for bread. A recent trend is to plant an aroma garden. After seeing a few, I added my own aroma garden, and the fragrance is especially pungent right after a summer rain. It is a delight for the senses.

More than one gardener has said that he or she foregoes an annual week-long vacation and instead finds daily renewal in his or her backyard garden. Most avid gardeners are happy to stay close to their gardens in the summer. Daily encounters with the garden offer abundant gifts in the form of rich sights, scents, and sounds; a connection to life; and the occasional surprise.

The gardens tell a story about where the gardeners envision themselves sitting to pause and enjoy the surrounding splendor. The flow of the garden evokes serenity and peace with careful placement of seating areas, a bench under a tree to provide shade, a chair with a tranquil view, or a sitting stone to enjoy the steady but quiet ripple of a water feature. One gardener who is also a botanical artist had her husband build an art studio with large glass windows in the center of her garden—a point of inspiration.

Another gardener showed me a special space in her garden that she had created for reflection. I started to wonder if I needed to create such a space in my garden and then realized that, although I do have seating areas, I use my whole garden experience as active reflection. I'm afraid if I created a special place to sit, I would fidget if I was sitting down and feel guilty if I wasn't. It was another reminder that each garden is unique, fitting the desires of the gardener.

Some gardens are designed to extend the living space of the home. The flow from inside the home to outside entertainment areas and garden rooms creates warmth and tells the visitor, "I honor my habitat as an extension of my home and of me."

The first time I heard the term *garden room*, I was intrigued with the idea that the garden could be organized into different sections, each with its own personality. One gardener even named her "rooms": forest room, desert room, sun room, and so forth. Colorado gardens that are designed to harmonize with the local environment tend to have lots of diversity. A garden I visited a few years ago was a great example of home and garden designed in synchrony with each other and with the surrounding environment. The home was designed in a Frank Lloyd Wright style that blended the architecture of the home with the sweeping natural lines of the garden space and open fields beyond.

A few years back, I visited an estate garden that incorporated a large entertainment center as a focal point of the landscape design. I envisioned large parties held in the lovely, welcoming sitting area, complete with outdoor kitchen and fireplace. When I asked about the spacious entertainment feature, the gardener explained that the special section of the garden was for the enjoyment of her family. Her garden story spoke of the importance of family in other ways. In one section of the yard, the gardener had planted unique species of roses (*Rosas*) that reminded her husband of his homeland in the Middle East.

Another gardener engaged her children in the garden story by designating a specific section of the garden for each child to create and tend. Each child selected a tree that was named in his or her honor. They helped plant and care for the trees, as well as the annuals and perennials planted as accents.

Some people are adamant that fairies are not real. Although I am not one to challenge the belief systems of others, I think it is a mistake to deny the existence of fairies. Not to believe in fairies is to miss some of the magic in the garden.

The garden is rich with opportunity for children to learn lessons about life and nature.

Perhaps as important, the garden also presents the opportunity to keep alive the kid still present in each of us. *Overheard in Fairyland* written by Bingham in 1909, is a book that was enjoyed by my grandmother, my mother, and later my sisters and me. It is out of print but can still be found online, thanks to the Baldwin Project. Mysteries in the garden are explained through story in a variety of endearing fairy tales, passed down from one generation to the next to quicken the imagination and entice little ones to develop a fascination with and passion to care for the gardens in their own lives.

Gardeners with imagination create small and large gardens for fairies to dwell. My friend Janean designed a grand home for her fairies. She landscaped a European village complete with pastures and sheep for the mysterious little inhabitants. Another gardener who participated in the tour created a railroad train garden, just the right size for fairies. An electric train chugs through miniature landscaped forests and grasslands. I was amazed to learn that there is a National Organization of Railroad Train Gardeners.

Sometimes, I have had to search for fairy lanes hidden behind larger shrubs and vines. Other times, I have spotted a raised dish with miniature trellises and chairs for the fairies. The options are as endless as the creativity and whimsy of the gardener.

This year, my friend Ann delighted visitors on the Greeley Garden Tour with an abundance of fairies and dragons inhabiting her gardens. Her daughter, transformed into a fairy complete with gauze tutu, was giving bells to intrigued visitors so they could beckon fairies. My five-year-old granddaughter, Cici, was suspicious and was adamant that she needed to see a "real" fairy, while seven-year-old Aleida wisely reported that she had indeed spotted a fairy floating on the back of a dragonfly.

In my world, fairies are akin to birds, bees, and butterflies, and I do what I can to welcome them all. Each spring, I study my yard to consider new places to insert birdhouses and new perennials that will attract winged creatures. Using a proactive approach to attract bees and birds to our gardens enhances the quality of life for a variety of living species. And who knows? I may attract a few fairies, too.

Greeley, like many other cities, has embraced the concept of community gardening. Most people think of community gardening as the opportunity to come together in a shared space while learning and practicing the art of vegetable gardening. True, joining a community garden is an ideal way to tend a garden if you don't have a plot of land or if you need the extra space to garden vegetables. The concept of community gardens is as diverse as the people who tend the gardens. In recent years, we have added a community garden to the Greeley Garden Tour. Invariably, visitors exclaim their surprise at the hidden gems in our garden community.

For example, one of our community gardens is designated for Weld Food Bank patrons so they can procure healthy produce. Another garden is designed to teach children from impoverished backgrounds to plant and harvest vegetables to share with their families. I visited a community garden that provides a learning opportunity for young men who are living in a sheltered home as an alternative to prison. The youth learn to plant, harvest, and prepare the produce from their garden. The concept of community gardens evokes images of vegetable gardens affiliated with churches, schools, and other nonprofit organizations. Most people don't realize that there is so much more opportunity in community gardening than just the growth and harvest of vegetables.

For example, in our community, we have a demonstration xeric garden that illustrates, through a self-guided walk along a shaded path, the rich diversity of plantings that thrive in the Colorado High Plains habitat. Houston Gardens in Greeley is a community garden located on seven acres on the corner of a busy intersection. It provides space for a large community vegetable garden but also includes a Colorado life zones nature walk, two ponds, a flowing creek, and a pollinator garden. This garden provides an oasis of serenity in the center of the city.

Recently, a woman I didn't know approached me, knowing that I am involved with the Greeley Garden Tour. She was ebullient in her description of a gardener friend who was in the process of creating a community garden in a rental complex through his gardening talents and giving spirit. I was intrigued and went to meet Ed. I recognized right away I was talking with a gentleman who has passion, whimsical ideas for art, and a genuine spirit of building community through gardening. He plants spectacular pots interspersed with his garden mixture of cheerful annuals and perennials. Ed has a unique interest in creating garden art out of recycled twigs and garden debris. But what is really special about Ed is that he wants his neighbors to be proud of their yards, too.

When people rent a living space, they generally don't have an obligation for the upkeep of the grounds they occupy. But Ed's infectious optimism for beautifying his neighborhood inspires his neighbors as well.

Recent reports of a dramatic increase in shootings in Chicago have mobilized some members of the community to take action and take back their neighborhoods. The "large lots" program allows people to purchase a vacant lot in their neighborhood for one dollar if they are willing to transform the space. Eager participants in the program are growing vegetables and flowers, creating space for education and other community gatherings, and hoping to instill pride and a sense of belonging in otherwise impoverished residents of the neighborhood.

Projects can be found in cities all over the country that involve planting gardens in vacant lots. Research has demonstrated that planting gardens in urban areas results in reduced crime. Furthermore, gardens instill a sense of community and pride.

The garden story reveals the passion and values of an individual, a family, or a community. Each of us has the opportunity to create his or her own story in the garden. As you think about the garden as a story, it can be helpful to collect ideas and to make notes about what you like and what story you want to convey in your garden. The process of journaling can be especially helpful during this phase of creativity and self-exploration.

When I was studying to be a psychiatric nurse, I learned about journaling as a tool for self-discovery. In some forms of therapy, clients are encouraged to identify their innermost feelings and write about them. I practiced that habit myself for a while with poor results. I dutifully scribbled all the dark and bright feelings from within, but then what? Having them on paper didn't help me. There wasn't any growth or change from that exercise. While there is certainly benefit in verbalizing or journaling one's dark thoughts and feelings, there is the downside of staying stuck. For example, it would be dismal to record all the problems that need to be fixed in your garden. Instead, allow yourself to dream and to explore. You are on a new journey, and you will create the elements of your story based on your values and beliefs.

I am suggesting journaling with an intention for the growth of *new* ideas. My belief is that, as you develop observations about your garden, you will make observations about yourself. For example, think of yourself and your garden as a story. What is your setting? Who are the characters who are already there? What do you learn when you pause to take in your living space? Where do you want to see change, new energy, or perhaps something to draw light or contrast in your garden? It is not uncommon for me to have a new idea pop into my head while I am in the midst of clearing a space in my garden. I have allowed room for new growth in my mind, as well as in my garden bed. This morning, while clearing a section of weeds, I worked through a knotty problem in something I was writing. Those are the ideas I like to journal.

There are lessons in the garden that facilitate self-discovery. At the end of chapters two through ten of this book, there are blank pages for journaling. I have provided questions to help you get started, but think of the questions as prompts to guide your journey. Your journal gives you an opportunity to record your experiences in a way that makes sense to you.

## JOURNAL PROMPTS

- Identify gardens you have visited that have inspired, surprised, charmed, or calmed you. In a few words, capture the story embedded in each of those gardens.
- What do you value most in gardens that you visit?
- Dream a bit. Sketch a garden that will tell a story about you. Tell the story incorporating your values; the setting of the gardens; and the trees, shrubs, perennials, and artifacts that could become characters in the story.

# Three

## Galloping Garden

*A garden is always a series of losses set against a few triumphs, like life itself.*

—MAY SARTON

I would like to say that I have a natural talent for gardening and that everything I touch radiates a healthy, vigorous abundance of vegetation. That just isn't true. I have had some miserable times in the garden. I have learned most lessons in life through trial and error. This has been especially true of gardening. I can only hope that, through sharing my experiences, I can encourage others to plunge into the messiness and discover joy and opportunity in their own gardens.

When Walt and I first became homeowners, we quickly realized that our domestic responsibilities had doubled. We each worked full time, and now we had a home and yard to care for. No children yet. Luckily, we started out with a small home in Alabama that was already landscaped, and there was little to do other than maintain. We couldn't get into too much trouble with that assignment! The warm weather and ample rain left little demanded from us, other than mowing. When we bought our first home in Colorado forty years ago, I tried my hand at vegetable gardening and immersed myself in partnering with nature to engage in the seed-to-harvest experience. My neighbor JoAnn and I grew cucumbers, and in the fall, we made jars and jars of pickles. I remember how proud I was to display my full jars of pickles after an evening of canning. It turned out that counting the jars was much more satisfying than sampling the pickles. Our pickles were lacking something that would have put them in the category of delicious. The texture was limp rather than crisp, and the taste was odd. But they were fun to make. And for me, the laughter and friendship we shared while canning trumped a tasty pickle.

Walt and I were living a pretty simple life, but apparently, we were itching to bite off more than we could chew. We were still young and naive when we decided that we were ready to tackle a large piece of property in the country where we would be able to sprawl out and enjoy some privacy. We were clueless about landscaping. The two and a half acres that we took on were a High Plains habitat, with not so much as a shrub or tree occupying the borders. Alfalfa and wild grasses were the dominant life-forms, with some bull snakes, birds, and pocket gophers as inhabitants. Prairie—we had purchased our very own prairie. Did we appreciate the natural beauty? No. We dared to tame it into a water-hungry suburban yard.

Following what appeared to be the norm in our western town, Walt and I planted a large, thirsty bluegrass lawn. We thought we wanted to be part of the American ideal, members of the "lush green lawn club." What we envisioned as space for soccer games, volleyball matches, and family celebrations became instead a hungry green monster that required endless mowing, watering, and fertilizing. We repeated the cycle over and over again. We also kept about an acre of pasture grass that we mowed during the summer. We didn't think much about the time spent in senseless lawn maintenance. We were focused on moving our family and our careers forward. There was little time for reflection on what we were doing in our yard.

Armed with a landscape design from one of the local nurseries, we planted the always-popular Colorado aspen (*Populus tremuloides*) and evergreen shrubs on three raised berms that curved around the maintained grass that surrounded our home. I described our landscape plans to my mother, and she was puzzled, since she had never heard of a berm before. A raised and shaped garden space was not part of a landscape plan in the small northeastern town where I grew up. The idea of berms, suggested by our nursery consultant, added interest to the landscape and would allow the leaves from trees to drop on the garden floor of the berm rather than all over the yard. It sounded like a good plan to Walt and me, and we were happy with the notion of less cleanup in the fall. Since then, I have learned that berms can be a big maintenance problem because of drainage issues.

On the east side of our home, we planted several showy mountain ash trees (*Sorbus decora*). We expected that when they grew, they would provide shade and privacy for us, as well as berries for the birds. The trees were adorned with fragrant white blossoms in the spring and radiant orange berries in the fall, a feast for the birds and other pollinators. Those trees were sure wonderful while they lasted. The average life span of a tree in North America is eight years. I didn't know that fact when we planted trees on our property, and I didn't understand the importance of planting trees that were particularly well suited to our environment. More on the plight of my showy mountain ash later.

We did like the berms of earth that provided areas for shrubs and trees to develop a discrete habitat separate but adjacent to the lawn. But I quickly deviated from the landscape design, which included a few simple trees, shrubs, and columbine (*Aquilegia caerulea*). I impulsively bought beautiful, exotic annuals and perennials, not knowing whether they were intended to survive in our environment. I didn't pay any attention to the recommendation of the Colorado State University (CSU) extension service: "right plant, right place." The advice is simple but effective. Plants that are adapted to the High Plains environment—when planted according to directions for light, water, and space needs—will thrive. I spent years of trial and error by planting, removing, replanting, and sadly watching the miserable outcome of my endeavors. I recall planting a burning bush (*Euonymus alatus*) in the same spot, only to watch the species wither and die not once but three times. I have since learned that it is difficult to grow much of anything at the base of a spruce tree (*Picea pungens*). Those pine needles make the soil very acidic. I guess the mantra I learned as a kid—"If at first you don't succeed, try, try again"—prevailed in spite of repeated failures. As mentioned earlier, the lesson "right plant, right place" wasn't considered as I deviated from the design. I was frequently taking on more than I could handle, and the notion of balance was nonexistent. I was building my garden without a compass.

I apparently had a knack for knocking myself out planting new areas in the garden, only to turn around and face patches of gigantic weeds that seemed to be stalking me! To make matters worse, my passion for vegetable gardening persisted in spite of a lack of time. When Walt and I lived in a small home, vegetable gardening was my only real garden responsibility. That, of course, all changed when we moved to our dream property in the country. In my already overscheduled and harried life, I committed to planting a big vegetable garden each summer. Walt is a man who scorns vegetables, but he was always happy to get the rototiller out to grind up the soil. When our children, Dave and Juli, were little, they loved helping me plant, tend, and harvest our vegetables. We were cheery and full of enthusiasm in the garden at the beginning of summer and even into the beginning of the harvest. To prove it, I have old photos of me standing in the garden holding a zucchini the size of a small child. One summer, I even fried zucchini blossoms. That was cool until Juli found a bee at the center of the crunchy delight. Every gardener has a zucchini story.

As Dave and Juli grew, their interests extended beyond the boundaries of the garden. Summer activities took precedence over time helping Mom in the garden. Assuming the role of summer taxi driver was the natural outcome for me. I would wave happily at other taxi moms, all of us driving wearily in circles. The once-pretty patch of earth went haywire. The notion of stepping into my garden to cheerfully dig and dwell in harmony with the outside vegetation turned into a dreaded and dreadful ordeal. I recall telling a friend that if vegetable gardening required a license, mine would be taken away.

While Walt and I were raising two kids, working full time, and squeezing camping trips into the mix in the summer, our yard suffered and became overgrown. Did I say overgrown? After ten years of what I would call benign neglect and an absence of intentional garden time, overgrowth was an understatement. Ground cover that once bloomed in small patches sprawled across unsuspecting shrubs and wove an unwelcome green web, interspersed with a bountiful crop of weeds. We fought not just weeds but grasshoppers and drought. We were even at war with the now-overgrown shrubs and perennials that we had once enjoyed in our yard. What had become of those tiny, tidy, manageable plants?

Walt and I looked at each other with a mixture of despair and a desire to kill. Really! What had started as several berms—which I tediously planted with small aspen (*Populus tremuloides*), evergreen shrubs, and assorted perennials—resulted in a jungle of weeds, shrubs growing within shrubs, and unwanted volunteers, steadfastly waving their green banners. I learned that obliteration is sometimes necessary for new growth to appear. Yep, a clean sweep is sometimes needed to find renewal of life.

We had found the time to build. But without a compass or realistic perspective, the outcome was dismal. I didn't follow our landscape plan and was certainly not intentional in my gardening activities. Hard work resulted in the need for more hard work. The solution to the yard was pretty straightforward: start over.

One of the saddest losses in our landscape were the showy mountain ash trees (*Sorbus decora*) that provided privacy along the side of our home. I could tell something was dreadfully wrong when the growth at the end of the branches rapidly died. We called a tree specialist to take a look and provide a remedy for the unknown malady. To our dismay, the trees had acquired a disease called fire blight. We had never heard of that problem and had no idea how our trees had developed the bacterial disease. We learned that apple trees that were growing in the neighborhood were likely infected, and there is a transfer that occurs from apple trees to showy mountain ash. We were sick. There was no way to save the infected trees.

The next to go was the bluegrass. I didn't feel badly about giving up our thirsty green monster. The variety of Kentucky bluegrass we had planted thirty years ago wasn't adapted to the harsh Colorado summers, and it demanded water that is much better placed on the farm fields. An abundance of weeds was choking out the bluegrass. I started to read about lawn options that were waterwise and congruent with the prairie around us. The research on hardy lawns for western gardens has been ongoing. There are some excellent options now for bluegrass and tall fescue, but at the time we were renovating our landscape, our options for waterwise grass were limited. We realized that the first step in starting over was removal of the thirsty bluegrass.

The berms were another story. The gobble-dygook of green that had once been identifiable shrubs and perennials had no beginning and no end. What could we do but scorch? And that is what we did. Seriously. There was too much to weed by hand, and the notion of spraying large areas was environmentally unsound. It became necessary to be heavy handed to gain control of the situation. Tough as it was to do this, it was freeing to take out the tangle of weeds that robbed the plantings of their form and beauty. My husband was the flamethrower, and I wielded the hose to douse the flames when they started to lick the trees. We did want to save the aspen trees (*Populus tremuloides*). I was actually able to create paths through the remaining healthy shrubs and gain a new perspective on the berms. One of my gardening friends coached me in making paths that had a destination instead of dead-ending somewhere in the middle of the berm. I could actually tour the gardens I created, and the new paths gave easier access to maintain my plants.

I finally started to take a class here and there about gardening with an emphasis on plants that would thrive in our climate and region. What a concept! Once I started to read more and pay attention to the groupings of plants in the local nurseries, I discovered something that became important for the transformation of my garden—and me. Plant types were actually grouped in the nursery according to their water needs. Eureka. Like people, plants thrive if they are allowed to grow in the right environment—for them. I finally understood the CSU extension service expression "right plant, right place." I quickly learned the fallacy of planting a shrub where I thought it would look good and instead learned about what the plant needed to survive and thrive.

I took a hard, honest look at the situation in front of me. I was humbled by my early gardening experiences but not defeated. I made a decision to start over. Time spent in the garden isn't always golden. I have sometimes learned best from dismal failures in my life. My gardening efforts were no exception.

But I knew there were alternatives to a trial-and-error approach to gardening and to life. I have observed that most professions have a stepwise approach to solving problems. For example, assessing or identifying the problem kicks the process into motion. As a nursing professor, I had practiced a formalized problem-solving process, the nursing process, throughout my career. I taught nursing students how to use this practical problem-solving approach to plan and provide care for their patients. Every plan of care starts with an assessment, a comprehensive overview of the patient.

In my everyday life, I sometimes forget to begin with an assessment of the situation. I become a "shoot, ready, aim" fixer, without gathering all the information needed. Even after identifying the problem, I sometimes forget to determine whether an action is needed. I find myself immersed in fixing a problem that doesn't need to be fixed. And when a solution is needed, I sometimes forget to consider the best action for the problem at hand. As I pause now before going to my garden,

I continue to learn and at the same time become more observant in my everyday life.

The building phase of life is exciting. Everything is new and shiny. But building homes, gardens, or careers without a plan can have long-term consequences that are filled with weeds. I enjoyed my early gardening endeavors, the thrill of planting, and watching new life grow and unfold in new and different directions. That enthusiasm carried me on a wave of good energy for a long time.

To my dismay, in the harried years of juggling family, work, and household responsibilities, my yard became an albatross—a burdensome plot of land to water, mow, weed, and water some more. Then, it occurred to me that I had much more than a yard or a plot of earth that was adjacent to my home. The living space around my home represented the possibility for changing how I worked and played. When I paused and looked at what was in front of me, I realized I had a garden that held a story.

I missed the early cues that my gardens were controlling me. Finally, I realized that I was in battle with my gardens rather than in harmony.

I remember listening to people talk about how much they enjoyed their gardens, and I glumly wondered what I was doing wrong. I felt chained to maintaining the out-of-control garden mess I had created, even though it wasn't working. It was a miserable place to be, but it was also the impetus to look for solutions.

I still sometimes dig into the maintenance aspects of gardening and life without stepping back to take a good look at what I am accomplishing with my efforts. I am continually reminded of the value of looking to the garden for guidance and then following a plan.

A natural outcome of pausing to learn from my garden was followed by the desire to be intentional as a gardener. I realized that having a plan that would be in keeping with the natural surroundings would guide me to care for the garden in a way that would be transformative.

## JOURNAL PROMPTS

- Take a walk around your garden, and pause in sections where you feel joy. What is it about this section of the garden that brings you happiness?
- Now stop by a section that has been a problem for you. What is it about this section that you don't like? Are there unhealthy or unwelcome species of plants, spots of overgrowth, or too many weeds?
- Describe as clearly as possible what frustrates you about this section. Have you always disliked this section, or has something changed here?

# Four

## Garden Gems

*We come from the earth, we return to
the earth, and in between we garden.*

*—Unknown*

My taste in gardening is eclectic. I enjoy visiting serene formal gardens; gardens with a
uniform palette of color; gardens that splash myriad brilliant, blooming clusters; and gardens that
incorporate the musical sounds of water ripples in
the background. But I also savor cottage gardens
and am delighted with whimsical and unusual

gardens. In the past ten years, I have developed a special interest in xeric gardens. And in the past few months, I have been uncovering the mysteries and value of native plants.

I started my gardening experience in somewhat of a haphazard manner, but I have developed my own style and now have a process that suits me. I have learned to appreciate a natural flow of vegetation, so the setting of my story mirrors the backdrop of the surrounding environment. Over the years, I have developed some strategies that make gardening a truly enjoyable experience for me. After more than forty years of gardening, writing more than sixty garden descriptions for our local garden tour in the past ten years, and taking numerous courses on gardening, I have developed a few insights.

One of the obvious rewards of gardening is new growth. As I write this, it is late summer, and I am in my fifth day of watering a hardy mix of buffalo grass (*Buchloe dactyloides*) and blue grama (*Bouteloua gracilis*) planted to surround an outbuilding on our property. Seeds were also sprinkled along a flagstone path that links the back of our home to the new structure that we are calling a barn—without animals. The barn is actually a combination of storage space on the bottom and play area overhead for our granddaughters, Aleida and Cici. Not a big fan of grass in general, I agreed to seeding the native grasses so that we can have a patch of growth to hold the soil and avoid a muddy mess in the spring. Anyway, after hand watering three or four times a day in the late-summer heat, I was rewarded this afternoon with a few sightings of sturdy little blades of blue green that sent my spirits soaring. I am a sucker for new life, and I find ample opportunity for celebrating the birth of new green stuff in my gardens. The renewal of hope when a seed pops is exhilarating, but there is another, larger prize that keeps me coming back.

As far back as I can remember, gardening has been a source of gratification coupled at times with extreme frustration. There is no other experience that allows me a feeling of joy as I stoop down and touch a little crocus (*Crocus vernus*) when it pops through the ground, while at the same time feeling frustrated and overwhelmed with the hardy crop of weeds that stubbornly embraces the little crocus. My garden helps me find balance. I also find my sense of humor when tending the garden and realize the insignificance of most things I worry about. I am energized and refreshed with even a little time in my garden. Oh, I get annoyed with the weeds and wasps. I think twice before going to the garden when it is intensely hot in the summer or walking in the garden when it is below freezing in the winter. So, what is the prize that keeps me coming back? It is the opportunity for transformation.

When I immerse myself in the garden experience and tend a plot of land, I realize that what seem like routine tasks yield an abundance of gifts. My work in the garden offers me an opportunity to observe, to feel less stress, and to develop my story. Over time, I have uncovered gems that have emerged from my time in the garden.

## *Roots*

When Walt suggested we move to the country to have space and privacy, I readily agreed. I didn't think about it at the time, but I was yearning for the space and room for adventure and play that was available to me as a child at my grandparents' country home. Environments that provided comfort to us as children are embedded in our memories. After all, those memories have emerged from our roots. There is often a conscious or unconscious yearning to re-create experiences and surroundings that provided joy and comfort.

Some of the plants I have selected are also reminiscent of my childhood. My mother and grandmother loved roses. A variety of hardy, colorful shrub roses (*Rosa*) make an appearance in several places in my gardens. I recall my mother's delight at the first sign of crocuses (*Crocus vernus*) and daffodils (*Narcissus pseudonarcissus*) in the spring. I practice the ritual of planting bulbs each fall, savoring the sweet surprise pop of color that heralds spring.

I have friends who have placed an old bicycle or wagon in the garden, and they use the structures as planters that evoke nostalgia for earlier times. My husband has an old stone wheel from a family homestead in Connecticut. The stone moved across the country with us and now settles as a backdrop for one of my garden beds. I grew up in the Northeast and knew that my grandparents and my mother found great satisfaction in planting bulbs and perennials. I was intrigued with the large vegetable garden that my southern grandmother tended. Over and over, I planted vegetable gardens for the pure pleasure of working in the soil and the joy of watching the zucchini do its magic. My roots have influenced my love of gardening, my perspective on what brings me pleasure in the garden, and my continual efforts in refurbishing and renewing the garden.

## Pause

First, I wake up. I don't mean that I wake from a deep sleep after a long night. It doesn't matter the time of day; there are many times when I am not fully awake to the experience I am living in the moment. To wake up is to be fully present when I go to my garden. That means tuning in to the world around me. I remind myself to take several deep breaths when I step outside. I look closely at my surroundings. And then I pause. Next, I consciously become aware of my senses. Tuning in to my senses is related to but not the same as meditation. I pay attention to what I see, the sounds around me, the feel of the vegetation around me, and, if available, the taste of an herb or piece of fruit or vegetable.

There are numerous articles about the value of meditation and, more recently, the practice of active meditation in the garden, which could involve active yoga or walking about a garden. There are books on meditative gardening and gardens designed for meditation. These are all indications that many of us yearn to reconnect with nature as an oasis in our chaotic and crazy world. Probably because I am by nature an anxious person, I have been interested in forms of relaxation and meditation as far back as I can remember.

I was introduced to meditation in the 1970s when I was in graduate school studying psychiatric nursing. I learned methods of meditation and relaxation and even completed a thesis studying the effect of brief progressive relaxation on anxiety in asthmatic children. Later, when I taught psychiatric nursing, I helped nursing students learn guided imagery and relaxation methods to help with the various stresses in their lives associated with returning to school and juggling multiple roles. Although I know that regular practice of relaxation and meditation works for many as a stress-reduction technique, I find a different renewal and connection to the earth when I am actively working in the garden. Immersion in the garden keeps me in harmony with the season and the health of my outside space. When my mind and body connect with the most basic needs of the garden, my whole being becomes engaged and then relaxed.

One day, as I was walking with my friend Kathleen, we were talking about our mutual love of gardening. She said one of her kids asked why she liked gardening so much. "It's because I disappear," Kathleen said. I can relate to that notion of disappearing or rather blending in with my natural world. When I am planting seeds, tilling the soil, or pulling weeds, I have random thoughts running through my head as I begin my activity. It takes practice to pause, to calm myself, to take deep breaths, and then to tap into my senses. Once I am more aware of what I am seeing, hearing, smelling, and sometimes tasting, the swirling mess of random worries in my mind starts to quiet.

Like Kathleen, when I step into the garden, I enter a timeless zone. I shed the encumbrance of a watch or clock and instead absorb myself in the needs of the garden at the time. For me, whatever I am doing in the garden takes precedence over the to-do list waiting for me in the house. I stop worrying about what is going to happen next and instead slow my pace. As my breathing grows quieter and my senses sharpen, I am ready to appreciate the sounds of birds and the fresh smells of the season. I become a character in the garden story.

I feel the air on my skin in the early morning in late summer and appreciate the cool temperature that heralds the beginning of autumn in a few short weeks. The shadows and sunshine spotlight different aspects of the garden, depending on the season and the time of day. This morning in late August, I rake the dry grass after mowing, and I stop to see the graceful movements of the ornamental grasses, trees, and shrubs as a cooling wind puffs across the plains. The landscape is forever changing.

Later in the afternoon, I water the new section of grass again, and I watch the sun set behind the old cottonwood tree at the back of our property. The orbs of light shining through the tree are like lights on a Christmas tree. The sharp cooing of mourning doves, startled as I come around a corner of the house, reminds me that I am not alone in my garden. The smell of rain comingles with the scent of cow manure, a signature aroma of where I live.

In Weld County, Colorado, the pungent odor of the local feedlot often comingles with the fragrance of my garden, especially in the spring when the soil is freshly tilled for planting and before rain or snowfall. Visitors joke about the stench, but I don't mind. The strong, earthy smells that are lingering in the air are part of the personality of my environment. The scents of my environment also become part of my garden story. I live in a large agricultural county that presents unique challenges to gardening. There are also plenty of rewards.

I take a taste of a tiny wild strawberry growing along my garden path. I smile at the memory of a class I took a few years back at a local garden center. The title of the presentation was "The Edible Garden." I was eager to learn about the shrubs, annuals, and perennials that are edible, as well as beautiful. Imagine my surprise when, after a brief introduction, the instructor walked us about the property adjacent to the nursery and started picking, nibbling, and passing around common weeds. I had no idea there were edible weeds. That was about the time I realized there was more to learn about gardening than could fill a lifetime. That notion excites me and challenges me to delve below the surface of the soil to learn what's going on down there.

I attended another gardening class and learned that when early settlers came to our country, they brought with them plants that they had found useful in the old country. One example is the plantain (*Plantago major*), a broadleaf weed that is plentiful in the fields around our yard and gardens. I view the plantain as an unwanted weed, yet it was useful as a soothing balm for injuries during the development of our country. The line that divides weeds from plants is decided by the perspective and values of each gardener. The story of the plantain and other plants brought to North America is changing. Plants that once served the needs of early settlers may be a threat to the ongoing survival of native plants.

When I pause in my garden and open the windows to my senses, I become immersed in a world that is bigger than a life bound by tasks and mundane duties. I look at my yard differently after I take the time to pause. The living space outside my home is welcoming and presents an opportunity for me to develop a story while I tend my garden.

## *Start over*

I have learned and relearned in my life that it is never too late to start over—with anything. My garden reminds me of that lesson every time I care to pay attention to the constantly changing activity there. When I was young, I held the naive idea that a landscape plan, once established, would remain more or less the same as a predictable arrangement of living species that would surround our home. I didn't consider the notion of transformation. My childhood home and yard stayed pretty much the same during my entire early life. People in our neighborhood didn't talk about water conservation or energy-efficient homes. But a lot has changed in the past fifty years in the way we think and the way we take care of our homes and gardens. Solar panels and other architectural adjustments are now available as options to improve the energy efficiency of homes. Xeric gardening was introduced in Colorado more than twenty years ago, with the intent of incorporating water-wise gardens throughout the West and Southwest. In recent years, there has been a growing movement to educate the public about the importance of native plantings.

Several years ago, our city water department participated in selling products dubbed "gardens-in-a-box." I purchased and planted one of those preplanned gardens that incorporated a beautiful variety of xeric perennials. I planted my garden-in-a-box in a section of the garden that had previously hosted barberry (*Berberis thunbergii*) and dogwood (*Cornus kousa*). The shrubs were not happy where they were planted, and their stunted growth and decaying structure guided me in starting over in that section of the garden. In a similar fashion, the newly planted perennials from my garden-in-a-box demonstrated pretty quickly which would thrive and which didn't care much for my garden environment. Some of the species did so well that I divided them and moved them to other sections of the garden. Others disappeared after one season of competing for a spot in my garden story.

Today, my gardens look very different from when we finished planting the recommended trees and shrubs in our first landscape design. Some of the changes are the result of disease or overcrowding. But many of the changes occurred as I learned and modified my beliefs and expectations of myself and others. I think about my garden story and how it is a reflection of the life I am living today. Do I want a high-maintenance garden that requires attention to detail? That would not fit the lifestyle my husband and I are seeking in retirement. I think about what brings joy at this stage of life. It is time with family and friends. I think about the children who are part of our lives and the dogs. I value a space that brings relaxation, beauty, and play space and requires minimal time and resources.

I honor water as a precious resource. When I garden, I consider the knowledge I have gained about xeric gardening to evaluate where I can start again. I look for patterns in the environment that feature families of shrubs that thrive in our environment. Species that will beautify the landscape with minimal water requirements are those that will become characters in my story. Furthermore, the native plants will be featured in starring roles as my garden continues to evolve.

## Garden with intention

The garden is a lot like a mother who loves her child unconditionally. My garden doesn't judge whether I am a prize-winning gardener. It thrives with some good soil, sunshine, a bit of rain, and some regular attention from me. In return, the garden provides me solace, purposeful work, and a glimpse of beauty in every season. Gardening challenges and changes me every time I allow myself to enter my garden with purpose, with intention.

My garden provides an oasis that quenches my thirst for solitude while I have a hand in the life that dwells in the soil beneath my feet. What I am doing in the garden is so absorbing that I am removed from my other world, which I like to call my cluttered life. In my cluttered life, I am caught up with self-imposed tasks and assignments that in retrospect seem trivial. My connection to the ever-changing garden story guides me in more meaningful work. Today, I make a decision to pull weeds to allow healthy plants and shrubs to thrive and spread.

> *I always think of my sins when I weed. They grow apace in the same way and are harder still to get rid of.*
>
> —*Helena Rutherfurd Ely*
> *"A Woman's Hardy Garden"*

I smile when I free my plants of the burdens of the weeds that are encroaching on their resources and space. I find a parallel when I consider my own "personal weeds" or character flaws. At times, my character defects choke out my positive energy.

Identifying a weed can be tricky. What is beautiful in one setting can be suffocating in another.

I turn my attention to the garden for guidance on what to tend and what to pull. If I pay attention, my garden guides the process of my activities. Intentional gardening spills into intention into my day-to-day life and keeps me in balance.

I take a close look at my shrubs and perennials. Some are brand new, some are a few years old, and some are approaching forty years. I am forever finding clues from my garden—to subdivide and move plants that thrive in my environment, to remove dead vegetation, and to revive plantings that are suffering from any number of maladies. I thin and give cuttings to friends to create space for shrubs to spread.

I have learned that when I enter my garden with intention and with curiosity, rather than an expectation of tasks to be completed, I am aware of the abundance around me and am humble in the recognition that I am just one member of my living garden community. I have visited many gardens in recent years, and I have observed that gardens in their multitude of forms, when tended with intention, bring a lot of joy and meaning to the life of the gardener.

I have a favorite quote from Ralph Waldo Emerson in my study:

What is success?

To laugh often and much; to win the respect of intelligent people and affection of children; to earn the appreciation of honest critics and endure the betrayal of false friends; to appreciate beauty; to find the best in others; to leave the world a bit better, whether by a healthy child, a garden patch, or a redeemed social condition; to know even one life has breathed easier because you have lived. This is to have succeeded.

I have the quote where I can see it every day. I take solace in the notion that I don't need a grand garden. All I need is a garden patch, a piece of land to tend and to learn from. I am intentionally gardening with the knowledge that I am leaving my garden patch to those who tend my garden after I am no longer here. Now that I am seventy, I have a keen sense that I am here for a limited time, but the garden endures. What I do in my garden can have a ripple effect for generations. The everyday tasks in the garden are no longer mundane. I like to think I am adding to the quality of life for future generations of people, plants, and pollinators.

When we moved to our acreage in west Greeley, we had a wonderful view of the mountains, and we didn't want to interrupt the magnificent horizon carved with the purple white-capped mountains. Now we are realizing the value of properly placed trees in the cooling of the property. The shade from the trees is functional not just for our family and friends but for all the species that visit our yard. I realize the trees may not even provide much shade while we are living here. But I like the idea of creating shade and comfort for those who will live here after we leave.

When I pause to become aware of my surroundings through all my senses and I am intentional in my garden work, I become aware of my inner creativity. I am more likely to develop new ideas for my garden and for my own life as well. I am able to develop a story that begins with me but extends to those who will follow me.

## *Partner with pollinators*

My primary role as a gardener is to tend my garden. I used to think of tending a garden as raking or weeding. But the act of tending is so much more. I am the director of the story, the caretaker, and the overseer. Tending the garden requires me to be alert to the others who are with me in the care of the garden. Pollinators are partners in my gardening endeavors. In fact, without pollinators, I wouldn't have a garden to enjoy. A pollinator is the critter that moves pollen from the anthers of a male flower to the female stigma. Pollinators are an important part of the garden story for a variety of reasons. They fertilize and allow our garden species to develop and thrive. Pollinators are key to the survival of our ecosystem. They form communities or networks that work together to assist in the survival of plant communities. Bees and butterflies come to mind as the most common pollinators. But there are numerous other garden helpers, such as pollen wasps, beetles, birds, and bats. The garden story is as much about the pollinators as it is the blooms that attract them.

When I invite company to my home, I pay special attention to my garden. I want the garden to be welcoming, and I want the colors and textures to stimulate the senses. But I am also intentional in designing my garden for the wildlife that depend on nutrition from blossoms for survival. In recent years, I have become so much more aware of the multitude of life-forms that visit my garden to seek shelter, to find nourishment, to pollinate, and to propagate. I am acutely aware I am but one tiny member of the world around me when I step outside my home and into my garden. There are many creatures that share the space I love, and I really want to learn who they are and to respect their time and place in the habitat we share.

There are certain things we can do to attract pollinators to our gardens:

- Plant native species. The CSU extension service has identified plants that require minimal water and do well in the West. Recommended plants are labeled as "plant select," which is a helpful resource in selecting new perennials that are waterwise.

However, these plants are not necessarily native. The Colorado Native Plant Society does provide a list of resources that are considered native.

- Plant in clumps rather than individual plants. Pollinators are more likely to be attracted to a mass of color than to individual plantings. The appearance of mass plantings is also appealing to the human eye.
- Intentionally plant for blooms throughout the summer. Look for preplanned gardens-in-a-box that are available through city water departments and nursery catalogs. Evaluate the products to determine if they are made up of native species and if they provide blooms throughout the spring and summer.

Planting a variety of trees and shrubs adds interest, but more important, it minimizes the incidence of a disease that can spread and destroy an entire species. Diversity in my perennial beds adds beauty, movement, and a wide selection of food sources for wildlife.

We feed the birds year round, and I am starting to learn the names of some of the visitors that frequent my garden. In recent years, experts have questioned the practice of backyard feeders, but we use seed blocks to minimize the risk of disease that can occur with stale food left in feeders. We have added a few new birdhouses each year and selected new shrubs for their appeal to birds. Likewise, I select perennials for their ability to attract pollinators. With some intentional caring from me, the garden is a petri dish for the basic life-forms that sustain all of us.

Mindful that the birds, especially the jays, would still want to visit the blooms of sunflowers (*Helianthus annuus*) once I removed the overcrowded stalks from one of my garden beds, I found a perfect spot by a split rail fence to move the stalk of a sunflower that volunteered in an inconvenient spot in my garden. Yesterday, as I moved sunflowers to areas where the seed would take root for next year's crop, I heard the loud *whoosh* of a hummingbird as it brushed past my ear. For the past several years in mid-August, I have been thrilled with the sighting of a hummingbird that comes to take nourishment from salmon-colored giant hyssop (*Agastache foeniculum*) blooms. I am intrigued by the important work of hummingbirds. They are doing a job that is essential for my survival and the survival of other forms of life.

The pull to my garden is irresistible. As the days turn to spring and summer, I must be outside to plunge my hands in the soil. The dirt under my nails is a reminder of my connection to the soil. It isn't a matter of planning to work in the garden when I am at home with free time. Rather, it is an obsession to get outside, to immerse myself in the messiness of the growth in my yard, and all the while consider the messiness and tangles that are embedded in my own life. The nursery rhyme "Mary, Mary, quite contrary, how does your garden grow?" comes to mind, and I smile. I am growing with my garden.

Transformation is the outcome of the lessons I have learned, found in the following gems:

- Honor my roots.
- Pause to wake up my senses.
- Look for opportunities to start over.

- Garden with intention.
- Partner with pollinators.

Where and how does transformation occur? It begins with the shift in my perspective of the world around me. I am a director of my story when the situation demands that role, but I am also a participant in the living, changing drama that surrounds me. I learn new information when I listen, and I develop sharp observation skills and patience. I use each of the gems and more as I pause, immerse myself in my garden, and become intent on telling my story.

Transformation is continually happening in my garden when I pay attention. Last year, my granddaughters, Aleida and Cici, learned about metamorphosis in the butterfly. Their aunt Juli gave them a kit complete with larvae so they could watch the process. The experience of watching the larvae cocoons develop and emerge days later as beautiful painted ladies was an early lesson for the little girls about transformation. It was also a reminder for the rest of us about the ongoing cycle of transformation in the life in our gardens and in our own lives as well. Now when we spot a painted lady meandering her way through our garden, seeking nourishment, we have a new appreciation for her life cycle and her contributions to the garden.

To tend a garden is to nourish oneself. The garden, like life, has lessons embedded in the soil, the vegetation, and the wildlife that are drawn to nourishment there. As you read this book, you are presented with the benefits of self-nourishment through tending a garden.

What do you want from your garden experience? It doesn't matter whether your garden occupies a small piece of land around your home or you have a large acreage. Perhaps you don't have a garden at all but enjoy visiting the gardens of friends, or maybe you tend a plot in a community garden. You can find ample opportunities to visit and tend gardens whether you live in a city or in a rural area. The father of one of my friends now lives in a residential home for the elderly. Throughout most of his life, he loved to engage in vegetable gardening. He proudly told me that his son helped him plant radishes and strawberries in a small garden box situated outside his bedroom window, where he could be witness to the garden designed just for him. Why would people need to give up a passion for the soil when they move to residential living?

Time in the garden is not always fun. Some days are hard work. Some days are frustrating. Gardening and life are like that. But some days are joyful. And always, always, there is something new to see, to touch, to smell, to hear, and to taste.

Surprise and delight can be found in the garden every season of the year. I consider the lessons I have gleaned in the garden to be gems, for they have made the rewards possible. Each of the gems is presented in the chapters that follow as I guide you in the development of your own garden story.

**JOURNAL PROMPTS**

- What is the stage for your garden story? Describe the location, typical weather in each season, and size of the garden that you tend.
- What are some gems you have discovered through your garden experience?
- What are your priorities as you develop a plot for your story?

# Five

*Everything from kings to cabbages
needs a root in the soil somewhere.*

*—Woods Hutchinson
"Civilization and Health"*

Gardening is an integral part of my life. I find solace and joy in the sights, sounds, and scents around me and a time to dream. I often reflect on my life while working in the soil. For me, time in the garden connects me to my ancestors and the values that have endured through the generations.

I am the oldest in a family of three girls. My dad was a US Air Force pilot and died testing a plane when my sisters and I were all very young. At twenty-eight, Mom was the sole parent; at the time, I was six, Cathy was four, and Susie was eighteen months. My mother raised my two younger sisters and me in a traditional neighborhood in the tiny historic town of Shrewsbury, New Jersey, not far from where her parents lived. Our yard and garden meant nothing to me other than a place to play. The open flow between our yard and the neighboring yards was perfect for evening summer games of tag and hide-and-seek. Mom didn't complain about mowing the lawn with an old-fashioned push mower. In fact, she said she liked it for the exercise. I think she used that old mower to show off her independence to the neighbors. Or perhaps, like me, she wanted any excuse to be outside.

My childhood neighborhood in the 1950s was stereotypical, with a mom, a dad, and assorted kids in each family. At least it seemed that way to me, because my family did not fit the picture. My mom felt different being a single mom and did not want to be viewed as a helpless widow. She enjoyed caring for a small perennial bed of flowers in the back of our house and was proud that she was flexible enough to touch her toes and easily weed the garden beds. She loved the rose bushes (*Rosa*) that bordered one side of our home. She and her neighbor agreed to share the cost of the rose bushes that grew around the wooden fence that formed a boundary between our two homes. There were numerous photos in the family album of my sisters and me standing in front of those rose bushes. I would say the photos bring back happy memories, but that isn't the whole story. Mom told us our neighbor had the nerve to claim the bushes as his own when he sold his property. Mom was furious when the new neighbor cheerfully claimed pride in her beautiful yard, complete with rose bushes!

Mom had a special attachment to a little dogwood (*Cornus*) tree that was planted in the front yard when we moved in. It was protected at the base by a clump of ivy (*Hedera helix*). We all enjoyed the litter of baby rabbits that found cover there every year in early summer. My mother loved the end of winter in New Jersey and especially the flowers that signaled the beginning of spring. She taught us all to look forward to the little splashes of color that we called Easter egg flowers, the hardy little crocuses (*Crocus vernus*) that appeared next to the front door. The first blossoms of the season in New Jersey were indeed a refreshing break from the long, gloomy winters. The humidity in the Northeast and the acid soil make a perfect environment for a dazzling display of azaleas (*Rhododendron arborescens*), which are spectacular, showy bushes that appear in many landscapes along the Eastern Seaboard. I, of course, tried them in Colorado, with little success.

I think of my mother's father as I putter in my plants and make decisions about what to pull and what to tend. My grandpa worked long hours in New York City. But on weekends, he headed to the woods adjacent to his country home. I recall the special smells of the damp, decaying vegetation and the sound and feel of the crunchy, dry leaves and snapping twigs under my feet as we tromped through the New Jersey woods.

My grandparents' yard had a dozen apple trees (*Malus pumila*) that produced bushel baskets full of apples. The apples were so plentiful, however, that they dropped from the trees and rotted in the grass. Grandpa decided a good solution was to pay my sisters and me a nickel for every apple we picked up. A nickel went pretty far in those days. I could purchase a candy bar or five pieces of candy; with two nickels, I could buy a comic book. The three of us scraped the rotting apples from the ground and into a basket, slowly counting our profits. It didn't take long for us to look up at the trees bursting with apples easy for the picking.

Likely it was Cathy, always looking for mischief-tinged adventure, who pondered, "Who would it hurt if we were to fill the basket a bit more quickly with the large, firm apples?" The three of us agreed that picking up the apple mush was becoming a chore. We quickly changed our strategy and filled the baskets with the low-hanging fruit. When our task was complete, our wise grandfather quietly surveyed our work. We sat on the grass, somberly studying the clovers while listening to his notion of hard work and honesty. We never tried that shortcut again. I suppose an apple pie made by my great-grandmother Oma with fresh apples from those trees softened the sting of our crime.

Beyond the apple orchard was undeveloped wooded land that became our special forest of discovery. To this day, I still favor landscapes that include undeveloped sections of land, be it forest or field. Although Grandpa built us a playhouse in back of his toolshed, it was the mysterious smells, colors, and sounds of the woods that beckoned us to our imaginary adventure games.

My father came from Georgia, and his mother had a practical approach to gardening. She came from a poor family, and her garden was designed to feed her husband and three children. A row of pecan trees (*Carya illinoinensis*) in the front yard provided a bountiful harvest of nuts that she would shell and salt for the holidays. I recall how excited my sisters and I were when the bundle of nuts arrived before Christmas. My grandmother likely thought Mom baked with the nuts, but Mom left that for Oma to do. Instead, we all savored the pecans for nibbling throughout the holidays.

When my sisters and I were little girls, my mom wanted us to know our father's family, so we visited the small town of Monroe, Georgia, where our dad grew up and our grandparents still lived. The vegetable garden in the backyard yielded bumper crops of summer produce, including okra, collard greens, and corn. I remember sitting on my grandmother's back porch helping her snap beans. We looked out at the large, abundant vegetable garden that produced enough for the family and plenty to share. It was heavenly to be in the comfort of her gardens that were so directly linked to her kitchen table.

The climate, soil, and vegetation in Greeley are strikingly different from those in the Northeast or the Southeast. When I started to garden, I needed to learn new ways of thinking about what would grow and thrive, particularly when it came to a limited resource, like water. As with life, my gardening efforts have had their ups and downs, successes and failures. I yearned to repeat positive experiences associated with gardening back East but had to learn the nuances of gardening in the West. I had a lot to learn.

It took me many years to stop, take nourishment from the garden, and pay attention to the lessons embedded in the soil. Recently, I learned that a primary source of nourishment for a plant comes from the tiny root hairs deep beneath the soil. I have also learned that 80 percent of problems that arise in the garden are because of poor soil. The power of the earth to nurture and sustain the garden is much like the power of the family to nurture and sustain its young.

The garden teaches me that attention to the roots and soil is paramount in the garden. The plants I have tended over the years have represented a mixture of species purchased from nursery stock and gifted transplants from friends' and neighbors' gardens. I have wondered at the resilience of some plants, while others seem so frail and vulnerable to disease and damage. The answer was always there in the roots, in the soil, in the very foundation of the plant. Early attention to providing the best beginning possible is an important take-home message. It is apparent that children thrive in the loving attention of their families, and the same is true for the various forms of life in our yards.

Gardening offers a series of problems to solve. One of the lessons I have learned as I tend my garden is that the opportunity to solve my garden problems helps develop my problem-solving skills for some of the bigger issues in life. When I was young, I could become discouraged by problems in my cluttered life, and I worked to eliminate rather than learn from them. I have come to believe that it is not the problems we have in life that define us but rather how we approach them. When I am an intentional gardener, I find a template for how to live life. Gardening allows me to connect to my roots, to touch and appreciate the mysteries of the earth, and to reflect.

But my garden is not a chunk of land to be tamed and sustained. It is a haven in good times and bad. I have found solace in my garden during some significant life events. Several years ago, I received a call from my sister Susie that our mom was in a coma and was not likely to survive. I had trouble breathing when I heard the news and had to sit down to grasp what was happening. Yes, my mother was old and frail and ready to die, but I was still shocked that she was leaving *now*. I felt a strong urge to be outside. At first, I just stood looking at the space of land around me, not able to hold a single thought. I couldn't take in the scents and sights that would provide comfort. Walking aimlessly around my yard eventually calmed me. I found a place to sit where I could stare at the sky. My breathing slowed, and I started to notice what my garden was offering. I smelled the scent of lavender and fresh grass. I felt comfort that the shrubs and the trees were steadfast in their reach to the sky and set in their sturdy foundation of roots—a reminder that there is a living world outside of and bigger than me.

The garden has been a place of solace on happy occasions, too. One early summer evening in 2009, our son, Dave, called to tell us that our first grandchild was on the way. I was out of my skin with excitement and anticipation. I stayed awake all night waiting to hear news of our granddaughter's birth. I talked with my daughter-in-law, Denise, before midnight, and we tearfully discussed the irony that Aleida June would be born on June 1. She would share the birthday of her grandma June, who had died of cancer just a few years earlier. The hours stretched on, and my mind raced with all the what-ifs. Silent prayers to Grandma June couldn't hurt. Light was beginning to ease into the room, heralding dawn. I had still not heard from Dave. I started to get anxious. I went outside, sat down on the bottom step of the deck at the back of the house, and let out a deep breath.

I started to journal as I watched the sunrise. The pink and lavender hues of the sky cast a rosy glow on the top of Long's Peak. I could hear the soft crinkle of the leaves, the birds chirping, and roosters in the distance. I felt a cool spring breeze that carried the scents of lavender and thyme. My senses were heightened with the anticipation of what was to come. I felt a connection to my unborn granddaughter and to the world she had yet to experience. I took a deep breath and studied a green leaf that had dropped at my feet. When I looked closely, I discovered it was actually a pretty shade of red. Why had I seen only green on my first glance? I wondered what else I had missed in nature by not pausing in my overly scheduled, cluttered days. I think back to those times in the garden with gratitude. I never feel so connected to death and to life as I do when I am in my garden.

I have been taking courses to continue my education about gardening. The power of the soil as sustenance for vegetation is paramount to a healthy garden. Although I was vaguely aware that it is the roots' job to help stabilize the tree to keep it from toppling over, and I knew that watering roots was important to keep the canopy alive, I didn't know that the soil needs oxygen to keep the roots alive. Caring for the soil over and around the roots is essential to sustaining the life of the tree.

Just as the roots in one's family set the stage for all that is to come later in life, so the quality of the soil affects the beauty and robustness of the landscape. Amending the soil with 5 percent organic material before adding any plant materials to the landscape will enable the gardener to have a successful garden with little maintenance. Of course, many gardeners are living with a landscape that has already been established. If that is the case, the gardener needs to be prepared either to live with vegetation that has less-than-optimal growth or to select plants that are adapted to poor soil. Creating the best foundation possible for growth and adjusting to the situation in front of us are lifelong lessons.

## JOURNAL PROMPTS

- Describe memories of your childhood garden or the garden of a family member or friend.
- Take a walk around your garden and identify aspects that reflect your roots.
- If you don't see evidence of your roots, is there a section of your garden that would be enhanced by vegetation or artifacts that are reminiscent of your past?

# Six

*In the depths of winter, I finally
learned that within me there
lay an invincible summer.*

—Albert Camus

The winter season as described in poetry is often accompanied by images of death. Numerous poems, essays, and photos depict the season as dark; gloomy; and, well, *dead*. I used to dread January and February. I blamed those dormant winter months for creating gloom in me. Apparently, I am not alone. I learned that January 6 is one of the most depressing days of the year. Why? It's because of broken New Year's resolutions, financial debt, lack of light, and postholiday blues. I recall holidays when I was in my thirties and forties, after packing up the Christmas decorations, bemoaning the short days and the gray skies. I felt sad and lacked energy. I would count the days until January was behind me. I allowed the cold days, icy streets, and lack of sun to cloud my mood. In truth, I was not open to the beauty around me. I was not attuned to my senses.

The lack of light wore on my nerves as I slushed through snow and slipped on ice. At the time, I decided I was a victim of winter blues. To make matters worse, my skin broke out in eczema. I had an angry rash on my legs and arms and even my neck. For a brief time, I tried a treatment recommended by my dermatologist that involved time in a light box. I entered a little room—more like a closet—with radiant light streaming at me for a concentrated time. I didn't feel any better after treatment in the light box. I felt like an animal in a lab experiment. I wondered why the hell I was in that little room when I could be soaking up sun in the tropics. I know it works for others, but I was claustrophobic and did not find relief from what I decided was seasonal affective disorder.

Caretaking was the first lesson I learned in life. When I was a little girl, I got lots of praise for caring for my sisters and helping my mom. To the delight of my family, I gravitated to a caregiving profession. I was a nurse for more than thirty years. Caring for others was rewarding. But it also drained the spirit right out of me. I was proud to be a wife, mother, and nursing professor, but the self-imposed drive to be the best in all I did took its toll. I was living what I now think of as a cluttered life. There was so much going on in my world that I had a hard time keeping priorities in focus. The energy it took to support the needs of each member of the family, manage my responsibilities at work, and coordinate our kids' transportation and school and social activities was often overwhelming. There was no time for me in that scenario.

I was teaching nursing, and Walt was an administrator at the local community college. In addition, we were raising two young children. After arriving at home, I plunged into the world of my family with continuing caretaking responsibilities. Once Dave and Juli were in bed, my smile collapsed along with my tired body, and I had no energy for anything but sleep. Eventually, I realized that I needed to be kind to myself. Like a plant, I needed tending. I needed fresh air and sunshine. Yes, artificial light does help many. But for me, the natural light and time for myself were what I craved. When I started to take winter walks during lunchtime at work, I started to feel better.

At first, I thought it was just moving away from stress in the office that helped. It took a few outings for me to realize that there were more changes happening as a result of my being outside. I noticed that my breathing relaxed. There was something energizing about being outside. I started to recognize the beauty of the icy shrubs and snow-draped trees. They stopped looking like dreary skeletal statues; bony, scattered tree limbs; and clumps of brown perennials and shrubs, abandoned cocoons that once radiated color, fragrance, and movement. The winter is a time of slumber, and in a sense, I was slumbering, too. I was not in tune with the world around me or open to the sights and sounds of nature.

My sense of smell was likely the first to awaken me to the abundance of life in the winter. I smelled the fresh, piney scents of evergreens and then listened to the birds chattering as they foraged for food. Ironically, it was the winter months that first taught me the importance of being outside in my garden year round. My lunchtime walks at work extended to exploring my garden in the winter. This was way outside my paradigm of entering the garden during the seasons when work accompanies the pleasure offered by the gardening experience.

All that happened years ago, before I was retired. Today is a snowy day in early January. Loki and I exchange glances. "Should we or shouldn't we?" I think the dog's vote is no, and I realize Loki's ambivalence about stepping outside his comfort zone matches my own. It's cold and snowing out there, and it's comfy in my home. But I decide we both need a winter walk in the garden.

On first glance, the juxtaposition of January and garden doesn't make sense. What does one "do" in the garden in January? Well, it turns out there is plenty to do if you are a serious gardener, but there is also the opportunity to simply appreciate the natural beauty of the garden in winter. There are some surprises in store if you haven't developed a relationship with the winter garden. When I step out the door with the dog at my side, I feel the sting of the cold air on my cheeks, but I also feel a connection to the earth beneath me that extends beyond my feet breaking through the snow. Little tufts of gold grass push their way to the surface of the snowfield in front of me—a reminder of the life-forms at work below. I think about the little plants and bulbs sleeping beneath the soil. The seasonal cycles in the garden, the continuity and predictability of the flow of the seasons, and their impact on the garden and on me are comforting. When I pause to really study the winter garden, it occurs to me that the garden isn't dead after all. It is taking care of itself by sleeping.

The garden has its own time for all its life functions. Even now, when the garden appears to be asleep, it is caring for new life. With the patience of a loving mother, the garden nurtures the roots and young shoots under the protection of crusty snow patches and frozen earth. It is a mother with intention, unconditional love, and quiet nurturing that fosters an abundance of healthy growth and transformation under the blanket of earth and snow. Mother Nature has a built-in cycle of renewal and rest that naturally occurs with the flow of the seasons.

I snap out of my reverie. It suddenly occurs to me that I could throw myself in the snow right now and make a snow angel! I loved doing that as a kid. I pause with the troubling thought that I could break something. What if I can't get up? I don't rise from a lying position with agility as I used to when I was young. I pause, but not too long. What the hell? Cell phone in pocket (in case I need to call 911), I ease myself down on the bed of snow. I am lying flat now, looking up at the sky and relishing the cold snow under my warm body. I am not in a rush to make an angel. I am just grateful that I made it down here, and I feel alive in the snow. But eventually, I do start to flail my arms about in wide arcs to shape wings at my sides. Satisfied that I can still make my dent in the world, I gingerly make my way to a crouch position, grateful for those squats in exercise class, and manage to get to an upright position to examine my work. Well, there sure was a flurry of movement that took place down there; the chaotic patterns in the snow look as if a struggle had occurred in this spot. Perhaps some animals had been fighting for survival. I laugh out loud. After all, there is a struggle between "me" who yearns to be a kid and "me" who is a mature woman now, learning to accept changes in my body.

My reflection shifts to my life today. I wonder about the untapped desires and energy asleep inside. What will I experience in this new year that will bring hope, joy, and adventure to my life? Many years ago, Dave and Juli gave me a snow globe for Christmas. It sits on my desk, and every now and then, I shake it up. The little flakes create a whole new pattern when they are disturbed. Shaking that snow globe fascinates me and boggles my mind with the possibilities of rearranging something that looks solid and static.

The cold silence of a winter garden walk provides a welcome respite. The rambling thoughts that are so often churning inside are quiet. As I pause, I watch the world around me much more closely. When I look at the clean, white, untouched snow, I am aware that I have a blank slate in front of me in terms of my own attitude.

There is a raw vulnerability to the garden in the winter. It slumbers naked. The skeletal structures of trees and shrubs take center stage in their own dramatic presentation. While the cloak of leaves provides beauty and movement in spring and summer, and the brilliant gowns of gold, rust, and red create a stunning performance in autumn, the long, cold months of winter allow the bones of the garden to be the stars of the show. Stately pines and low-growing evergreens soften the stark, bold bones of the trees and shrubs. Each tree has its own personality, and winter allows that personality to become more visible. My gaze shifts from the towering pines to the tiny, tenacious ground cover hugging the soil that is exposed on the sunny side of the path.

As I study the evergreens in my yard, I notice the brown needles underneath. I used to worry that the tree was in distress, but I have learned that a natural process of shedding occurs yearly with pines and spruce. I once believed that conifer needles lived forever, but just as there is a life cycle for humans, animals, and plants, so it is with the evergreens. They shed needles every year. The yellow-to-brownish color that occurs underneath branches provides evidence that it is time for the needles to drop. It seems to me that all living creatures go through a shedding process periodically for new growth to appear. I am inspired to shed excess baggage from my own life when I appreciate the simplicity of the winter garden.

I tend to be controlling and not only manage my own life but also attempt (to a fault) to manage the lives of others. Once I give up the belief that I am in charge of the world around me, some of the results of my controlling behavior smack me in the face, and I realize I have a choice. I think about the snow globe that is static one minute and swirling with change the next. I have a choice about my behaviors. I can choose to be more at ease in myself and more at ease with others. I learn this lesson from the winter garden. Dormancy leads to new growth. I am grateful that my life is no longer cluttered but intentional.

I don't stay out long on a day that is bitterly cold with a blustery wind like today, but I stay long enough to realize that the outing was an opportunity for active meditation. I gave myself a gift with my winter walk. I smile when I realize I was kind to myself.

In Colorado, the weather doesn't stay the same for long. A snowy day is often followed by a day bursting with sunshine. Just one day after the snowstorm, the sun is brilliant. This morning, I started the day puttering in the house and took a short break to look out the window. The wind was swirling puffs of snow from the roof of the house. My mouth dropped at the sight of the full moon delicately placed between salmon-pink clouds swimming along the robin's egg–blue morning sky. I looked down and then allowed my eyes to trace the landscape around me, the winter palette. White, silver, blue, azure, mauve, taupe, gray, old-earth solid protective evergreen, mottled brown gnarly tree trunk, crusty brown crumb-cake snow mounds—they are the rich colors of winter. The myriad winter colors and their moods offer a time of reflection and gratitude.

It's time to get outside with the dog again and soak up some of this sunny winter morning. For some reason, the poem that begins with "What is so rare as a day in June?" pops into my head. Funny, I know. But not so silly when I realize there is a parallel between the frozen elegance of winter and the seemingly faraway beauty that enraptures us in June. After all, January also offers experiences that are rare. The proud, naked trees that allow us to admire their unadorned structure and the soft, pearly gray clouds that cast shadows of rose and blue on the patches of snow that blanket the grasses asleep below entice me to wonder, "What is so rare as a day in January?"

Today, Loki is romping rather than trudging through the snow. He moves clumps of snow with his paw here and there to examine the world beneath. The warmth of the sun is melting some of the snow today, and I muse about the impermanence of life and me. A few days ago, I traced the date in the snow on the bench where I sit in the summer to watch the birds. I wanted to check it out and see what had remained. The six was morphing into a loose circle. I traced an eight in the melting snow and could see that the number was already sinking into slush.

Thinking about the quickly melting snow, I am reminded that nothing is permanent. I feel somber and yet exhilarated when I turn the thought over in my head. I am here for a limited time, but my actions may actually have a ripple effect. What I do today to live with intentional kindness can make a difference this very minute. Research supports this idea. I can begin with the wildlife that surrounds me. It's important that I am kind to myself. That's a start. But how can I be kind to the birds in my own backyard? I can start by watching them at my feeders.

Numerous hungry birds flock to the seed blocks, full bird feeders, and water to quench their thirst. James Audubon spent his entire life studying birds, and his legacy is a challenge for us to better understand the behavior of the birds that share our habitat. I realize how much more connection I have to the life in my garden when I am better acquainted with species that share my space.

There is recent evidence that bird feeders may be attracting birds that are invaders rather than the native birds. Furthermore, feeders that are not cleaned regularly can be a source of disease for birds. As an alternative to feeders, the Audubon Society recommends planting trees and shrubs for protection, as well as food sources for native birds.

I am reminded to be patient, to be quiet, and to take a step back in my eagerness to learn about life in my garden. Although it is easy to watch birds at a feeding station, I can learn more about their behavior by watching them in their natural habitat. I pause. I am reminded of a quote from Emerson: "Adopt the pace of nature: her secret is patience."

When I walk through the garden at rest, I can see the vegetation from a different perspective. I notice that the garden is an important haven for birds all year long. More birds of prey appear on the tallest branches in the yard during the coldest months of the year. The tiniest birds peck for seeds and bugs all winter under the protection of the low-growing shrubs. I am learning that the garden is planted not for my enjoyment alone but as shared property for humans and wildlife.

Hard as it is for me to be silent, the winter season nudges me to get in sync with the muted sounds of the season. I am inspired by a quote from William Penn: "True silence is the rest of the mind; it is to the spirit what sleep is to the body, nourishment and refreshment."

Signs of spring will soon be apparent as the days get longer and snow melts. A relationship with the garden in the spring is filled with the heady scents and colors of fresh blooms, but I appreciate that experience all the more because of the commitment to commune with the garden in the dormant months of winter.

During a time when I was truly burned out, the garden renewed me, and I shifted my perspective on life. The garden has many gifts to offer, but the most significant gift for me occurred as a result of the actual process of gardening. When I took the time to tend a garden, I felt a huge relief from the burdens I was largely heaping on myself. This may be hard to believe, but time in the garden really did work for me. How did this transformation of perspective happen? One thing is for certain. It was not the result of completing tasks and certainly not the result of a perfect garden. In my cluttered life, rewards were often found in checking off lists.

The well-being that came from gardening happened because I gave myself a chunk of undisturbed time to engage in something that I enjoyed and that had meaning for me. The allure of being in the garden was initially the appeal of being outside and with nature. I have friends who will give themselves undisturbed time and meditate, play bridge, shop for clothes, or get a massage. Although I can enjoy those and other activities that pull me away from ordinary demands of life, my primary source of renewal comes from the experience of gardening.

## JOURNAL PROMPTS

- Identify places in your garden where you can pause. Give a name to your garden that describes the feeling you are trying to convey.
- Visit your garden on a quiet winter day and describe what you admire using each of your senses.
- Typically, your senses are heightened as a result of working in the garden. What have you noticed about yourself after you have spent some time tending your garden?

# Seven

## Start Over

*I think the true gardener is a lover of his flowers, not a critic of them. I think the true gardener is the reverent servant of Nature, not her truculent, wife-beating master. I think the true gardener, the older he grows, should more and more develop a humble, grateful and uncertain spirit.*

—*Reginald Farrer*
*"In a Yorkshire Garden"*

Starting over is scary because it involves changing things up. Change can involve a lot of time and resources. When it comes to landscape decisions, the thought of starting over can be daunting. But it is also exciting.

If I begin to feel stuck in gardening or in life, I remember there is always the opportunity to start over. I relish the notion that a story begins where we want it to begin. I don't need to continue with an experience or situation that is miserable. When I made the decision to end the cycle of caring for an out-of-control yard, I was liberated, and that decision completely changed my perspective about gardening. It was such a relief to stop behaviors that just weren't working. I could shed my old ideas, abandon the loyalty to the impulsive path I was following, and be open to a new plan that actually had focus and intention.

Our country property is two and a half acres. It has berms that separate the portion of our yard that has been landscaped from the larger portion we have left open to wild grasses with walking paths, so we can enjoy nature walks with the dogs. The taller shrubs and trees provide a woodsy border to the fields beyond. The natural setting on the eastern plains of Colorado had great appeal when we purchased our property more than thirty years ago. We still love the property that surrounds our home, and one of our priorities whenever we start over is to maintain and enhance the natural beauty.

As a gardener, I do have some choice about what lives and what dies. I now follow a plan, and when I purchase plants, I always look for water-wise plantings. I learned a long time ago in a class I took about perennials that it is pleasing to the eye to plant in uneven numbers and in uneven groupings. Nature has a rhythm that is artistic in its uneven placement of vegetation. The rich diversity of flowers and shrubs and the abundant variety of texture, height, and color are inspirations to me when I think about the design of and movement in my own garden.

The driving force in the decision to start over was the burdensome, wasteful watering ritual we followed with fierce loyalty and commitment. We and the other homeowners in our neighborhood bought water rights when we purchased our homes. We are members of an irrigation ditch that has access to water that travels from the mountains to saturate farmers' fields and then to our ditch. During the summer months, biweekly watering of yards and pastures is a way of life for homeowners in our neighborhood. The irrigation water is a great resource, but the watering ritual is a big commitment. It involves being home to turn the pond pump on and off to water your yard and pasture. We followed the watering ritual for years in the interest of maintaining our large bluegrass lawn. I couldn't help but think a lot about water when it occupied so much of our time during summer.

It started to occur to me that dumping water on large sections of bluegrass was wasteful. There had to be a better way to spend time and resources when it came to our yard. The first step in transforming our yard and garden was the acknowledgment that water is a precious resource.

Water in Colorado is a coveted commodity. Greeley is in Weld County, one of the largest agricultural counties in the country. Farmers depend on water for their livelihood. And we depend on the farmers for our food supplies. Until recent years, most homeowners watered their yards without much concern for the impact of global warming on our supply of water.

Some families still plan landscapes with thirsty vegetation, but that is starting to change. Increasing numbers of homeowners plan their landscapes with water needs as a guiding framework. Xeriscape, a term coined by the Denver Water Department in 1982, allows a wide range of design choices for the gardener. The basic idea is for the gardener to select plantings that are native and drought resistant. Native plantings thrive in cottage gardens; country gardens; mountain landscapes; gardens designed for entertainment; and naturalized gardens adorned with bulbs, wild grasses, and wildflowers. My Colorado garden has evolved to accommodate my increased commitment to saving our planet one garden at a time.

When I first started gardening, I was a novice. I didn't have a clue about the most appropriate species of trees, shrubs, and plants for Colorado. I would attend home-and-garden shows, stroll through nurseries and gardens, and become so overwhelmed I couldn't make sense of what was in front of me. I could empathize with Alice in Wonderland, lost and wandering in a giant garden maze. But unlike Alice, I wasn't overcome with wonder. I was just befuddled.

Walt and I have always been concerned about the limited resources that we are leaving for the next generation. We built our passive solar home in 1977 when we realized the power and resource potential of the sun in heating our home. The notion of incorporating xeric in our landscape redesign made a lot of sense to us. The first step was to recognize that our original landscape plan was no longer working. Once we realized that we were not chained to that plan, we were free to find and implement a design that would work for us.

I read everything I could about xeric landscaping, and I could see that there was an overarching philosophy to waterwise gardening. When I learned that the goal was to conserve water and at the same time beautify my surroundings, I was thrilled. The only plantings that go into the garden are those that thrive on the eastern plains with little maintenance or water. That philosophy made sense to me and would guide a redesign of my gardens. There are excellent resources for xeric gardening that are found at the back of this book, but the point is that I was intentional. I was following a plan that provided focus when I entered a garden center. I was gardening with a new perspective. There are seven basic principles that guide my efforts and produce lovely results in my garden.

While learning about xeric gardening, I started to focus my attention on garden centers and catalogs that featured waterwise and native plantings. During this time, I also found that I could still plant vegetables and herbs, but I had to group the plants according to their water needs. Conservationists describe this method of strategically placing plants as hydrozoning. The concept is simple and makes so much sense. Plants that need more water are planted in the same section of the garden. Plants that thrive in the shade are planted in the shade. Plants that enjoy dappled shade are planted in dappled shade. The expression "right plant, right place" mentioned earlier in this book guides decisions from purchase to placement in the garden. This basic concept says so much about the value of matching a plant to its best environment. Placement of shrubs, perennials, and annuals according to their water needs also makes a great deal of sense. I choose to hand water the herbs and flowers that need attention, so I place them close to the house where I can tend and harvest them more easily. Likewise, I am comfortable leaving the most robust xeric species to fend for themselves once established. I understood those two words *once established* much better once I started to pay close attention to the process of establishing new perennials and shrubs in my yard. New life in the garden requires extra attention and water to establish a good foundation. My plants guide me in their watering needs when I am able to pause and pay attention to their condition.

I would describe myself as an eclectic person. I have many interests, and that can be a good thing. But before I started over in my garden, my eclectic approach translated into a landscape that was missing its soul. Trees, shrubs, and plants were all there, but they were like characters in a play without a script. There wasn't a coherent story.

I turned to local experts for help. Most nurseries have an employee skilled in landscape design who will provide recommendations and assistance with starting over. I read a lot about xeric gardening and drew a rough sketch of what I had in mind before I approached a landscape designer from one of the local nurseries. I could finally visualize the big picture of what I was trying to accomplish. At the time of this redesign, we wanted to simplify our gardening efforts and also create a lovely series of gardens with waterwise plantings.

One of our first objectives was to remove all the Kentucky bluegrass (*Poa pratensis*) and plant a much smaller area with a combination of buffalo grass (*Buchloe dactyloides*) and blue grama (*Bouteloua gracilis*). This mixture is drought resistant but does have the disadvantage of greening up late and turning brown earlier in the fall compared with the neighboring bluegrass yards. It suits our landscape because we have a country property with wild grasses adjacent to our landscaped gardens. I have seen many xeric gardens in which the gardeners have eliminated a grassy lawn entirely and instead planted lush, varied gardens throughout the yard. Research is underway at Colorado State University to develop bluegrass lawns that are environmentally friendly. Families that want a green lawn can still have that, with a variety of choices that are congruent with the environment.

Because we decided to eliminate the bluegrass, we added new berms to border the yard where it had been. We were able to find free dirt, left over from a construction site. We hauled the dirt to our property and made a huge mistake by not amending the soil. I did not have a clue about the importance of good soil as a foundation for a healthy garden. Now I work compost into the existing vegetation, but the process is laborious once the landscape is established.

Next, we covered the large areas of dirt with a weed barrier because we knew we would be up to our eyeballs in weeds without some help. It turns out this was another mistake. The weed barrier does not allow the soil to breathe and benefit from the addition of soil amendments over time. Each year, I remove sections of the landscape fabric and amend the soil as part of the process. We added mulch, also free, on top of the weed barrier. The city trims trees in the spring and chips the limbs for residents to take for mulch in their own yards. The chips were rough clumps of wood, and occasionally I found assorted debris, such as crushed cans, in the chips. The area we were covering with mulch was huge, so we could tolerate the rustic mound of free chips. I now spring for a truckload of cedar mulch every two years, and I look for a grade of shredded bark that blends with our property but does not have surprises in the mix. The objective is to keep soil surrounding my plants protected by three inches of fresh mulch to keep moisture in and weeds out.

Before planting any trees or shrubs, we placed railroad ties as a border between the berms and the grass. Walt placed flagstones for a path around the house, and I followed by planting waterwise sedum (*Sedum hispanicum*) between the stones. The sedum spread easily with no water other than rainfall. The ground cover keeps the weeds out, and a lovely cluster of white flowers appears as a bonus each spring.

As for the sequence of planting on the berms, we started with trees and shrubs that were on sale in the fall. I quickly learned that fall was an ideal time to plant because the temperatures were mild, and the plants did not need watering as frequently.

When I was ready to plant perennials, I ordered some preplanned gardens that were entirely xeric. I also added a few garden-in-a-box products from the local water department. I dug holes according to the planting directions for each shrub and perennial and amended the soil where the plant was to be placed. I was fortunate that the species I selected thrived in spite of my patchwork approach to soil preparation. Many varieties of xeric plantings actually do better in soil that is not too rich. Planting the ready-made gardens gave me the confidence and inspiration to get started with hardy perennials before I branched out on my own to expand the diversity of my plantings.

I have had had some failures along the way. In the interest of removing yet more grass in our backyard, I planted a prairie garden amid my mixture of buffalo and blue gamma grasses. When I looked at prairie gardens in catalogs, the illustrations revealed colorful fields of blooms dancing on the wind that beckoned visitors to celebrate nature. I selected perennials that were xeric, and many were featured in the illustrations. I interspersed them among the buffalo grass (*Buchloe dactyloides*) and blue grama (*Bouteloua gracilis*) in the backyard. My bubble dream of birds, butterflies, and people dancing in the meadow popped in a sorry splatter of xeric blooms struggling in tall, thick clumps of grass. The section of the yard designated as prairie looked more like a giant mishmash of scraggly plantings that were invaders. I resisted starting over once again and allowed two years of growth before I transplanted the perennials to my berms, where they could be maintained without competition from the grass. As a long-term plan, I may try a prairie garden again, to add a splash of colorful surprise. But it will be in a section of the field adjacent to my landscaped yard. Even when there is intention accompanied by a plan, not every gardening decision works. The good news is that most plants survived and thrived once moved to a space where they were free to sprawl.

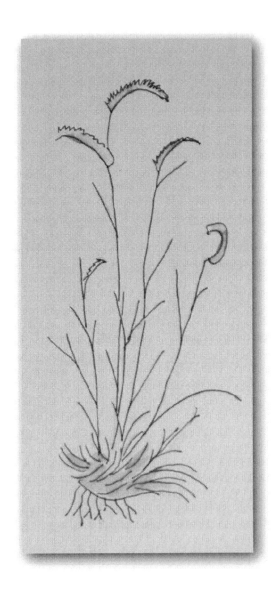

- Identify a section of your yard that is giving clues that it is time to start over.
- Identify the problems.
- Before starting over, pause and think of the big picture. What are you trying to create in this section of the garden? Consider diversity of texture, seasonal color, height, and space requirements. Identify the steps it would take to make a change.

# Eight

GARDEN WITH INTENTION:
XERIC GARDENING

*We never know the worth of
water till the well is dry.*

—*THOMAS FULLER*
*"GNOMOLOGIA"*

When I first saw the word *xeric*, I was intrigued. *Xeric* comes from the Greek word
*xeros*, meaning "dry." The term *xeric* was coined
by the Denver Water Department in 1982. The
premise of xeric gardening makes so much sense

to me because the goal is to plant vegetation that is adapted to the local environment. The average annual rainfall in the community where I live is 14.7 inches. It is important for me to be mindful of water needs of the plants that I include in my landscape plan.

Too many people misunderstand the concept of xeric. I have heard folks use the term *zeroscape* to describe xeric landscaping. A common misperception is to associate xeric gardening with a disdain for colorful perennials and anything green. Nothing could be farther from the truth. Folks who think of xeric gardening as gravel and avoidance of vegetation are mistaken. Trees, shrubs, perennials, and grasses that thrive with little water are abundant and interesting in texture, color, and form. There is, in fact, a huge selection for the gardener ready to plant a xeric garden.

My gardening story and redesign process continue. My husband and I are aware that our needs are changing as we age, but we want to remain in our home and are not quite ready to downsize. We are happy with the progress we have made in transforming our yard to a landscape that includes xeric trees, shrubs, and perennials. But it is time to simplify further. It is time to be intentional about the changes we will make in our living space, indoors and out. I continue to learn about xeric gardening, and this year I became a certified gardener through an online program at the Colorado State University extension service.

Our life story and garden story parallel each other and intersect by informing my husband and me that we need to make some changes that will cut down on the number of hours we labor in the yard yet enrich our gardening experience. When I follow the seven steps of xeric gardening, I have a plan that guides me in all my gardening decisions.

## Step 1: Planning and design

When we moved to our home in 1984, we had a design that we used as a template. We quickly deviated from the plan when I became intrigued with plants for sale in local garden centers. I was not aware of xeric gardening and was not focused on plants that would survive our hot, dry summers.

About ten years ago, we started over with a new design that would commit to xeric plantings throughout the yard. That was a huge endeavor but has had huge benefits in terms of saving money and eliminating wasteful watering. It was satisfying to be intentional about my gardening journey. I continue to follow the seven steps in successful xeric gardening and am committed to following a plan as I look for sections of my garden that need revision.

We have managed to live in our home for more than thirty-five years with kids, grandkids, and pets tromping through the yard. Until recently, we resisted fencing in our yard. When we bought our property, we relished the lack of boundaries, the wide-open space, the magnificent views, and the ample room for kids and dogs to romp. Well, we now have a granddog who loves to gallop beyond the natural boundaries that our previous family dogs accepted. Freye, when confronted with a rabbit, has a gait that reminds me of a gazelle. She leaps into the air, tears off to parts unknown, and returns on her own timetable. We have finally come to realize that Freye's need for exploration and our need for transforming our outdoor living experience came together in a plan that would work for all of us. It became apparent that it was once again time to revise our landscape. We have remodeled various sections of our home over the course of our lives. It makes sense to remodel the existing landscape as our needs and desires change.

I want my home and gardens to have unity, to have a theme that reflects the values of my family, and to tell a story. I started the current phase of landscape redesign with a sketch and a description of how I wanted to interact with my landscape. First, I considered how I wanted the space to be used. We have grandchildren, granddogs, and a dog of our own. We love to entertain. We have numerous bird feeders, seed blocks, and birdhouses to attract birds to our property. Yet I realized something was missing.

We discovered that there was a downside to the open flow from our yard to the field beyond. Like an unframed piece of art, the garden lacked a frame that could be created by a fence made of materials suitable for our landscape. Over time,

I discovered that the freedom that accompanied a lack of boundaries did not evoke a feeling of warmth. Adding a natural wood fence to a section of the backyard provided the frame that I wanted and a boundary for the dogs.

Another consideration was the lack of shade in our surrounding yard. When we built our home, we wanted to maintain our fabulous view of the mountains, so we did not plant trees in the yard, concerned that they would obstruct our view. Unfortunately, we were missing the cooling comfort and shade of mature trees. We also recognized that the lack of shade created a scorching backyard in the summer.

I am ready to create rooms where there was once an open garden flowing to the prairie. The addition of a fence that blends with the natural surroundings, the shade trees, and a seating area adjacent to the back of the home would be an intentional renewal of my garden experience. My long-term plan includes the addition of a rock feature, bubbling to a soft bed of pebbles below. It never hurts to dream as a part of the planning process.

## *Step 2: Improving soil*

Just as the family is the bedrock for survival of the young, soil is the most critical element for the health of the garden. The harsh conditions of western soil are challenging for the gardener unless the soil is amended with compost or other organic material. When I was a novice gardener, I did not pay attention to the importance of the soil. I have learned the hard way to understand and respect the composition of my soil before exposing any vegetation to its new habitat. I now know that my yard is composed of soil that is heavy in clay, with some areas that are largely sandy.

The recommended addition of 5 percent organic matter to the soil can make an amazing difference in the health and beauty of the garden. Soil amendments, however, vary greatly. A comparison of the range of selections available at garden centers reveals diverse offerings such as horse, sheep, or chicken manure; rubber; garden debris; and other assorted amendments. Some composts include nutrients such as nitrogen. Nitrogen is not beneficial for most species of native plants in Colorado. On the other hand, mycorrhizae in the soil are important for native plants. These magic wonders are the microscopic organisms that enrich the soil and provide oxygen. Oxygen in the soil is also essential for plants to thrive.

I have learned that the simplest solution in life is often the best. Compost made from yard and kitchen scraps is not difficult to create or apply, and the process of recycling natural resources is gratifying. I have a compost pile in the backyard and keep a container by my sink to collect vegetable scraps. I layer grass clippings, dirt, and kitchen scraps; water occasionally; rotate the pile; and add the homemade compost as needed to amend my garden bed.

The vegetable garden and the perennial beds flourish with a renewal of organic compost each year. One gardener friend with spectacular perennial blooms cuts back her blooms in the fall and leaves just a few stalks of plants for winter interest. Then, she applies bags of sheep and peat compost over her beds and allows the magic formula to seep into the soil during the winter snows. The results in the spring are amazing.

We placed landscape fabric over our entire garden area several years ago, and now I have learned that there are many problems associated with having a barrier that covers the soil. The soil underneath stays hard and compacted and lacks the richness of soils that are amended. I have gradually been removing the fabric, gently digging in compost to enhance the soil underneath, and have already seen some great results.

If the soil is not amended when the garden is created, it would be wise for the gardener to select plants that will thrive in poor soil conditions. Fortunately, many species that have their origins in the West thrive in poor conditions.

I have enjoyed experimenting with a variety of drought-hardy perennials. Most are right at home in the challenging soil conditions.

## *Step 3: Create practical turf area*

When I first learned about xeric gardening, I had the mistaken idea that grass was bad. When visiting the gardens that will be featured on the Greeley Garden Tour, I see that I am not alone in that belief. Many homeowners are committed to reducing grass and replacing it with waterwise perennials and shrubs. I have seen some lovely gardens with little or no grass. But I have also visited yards that resemble parks in their design of grassy areas accompanied by shaded seating. I have learned it is not the grass that is the problem; it is the way the grass is watered.

The design process described in step 1 guides the configuration of grass, garden, and seating areas. What is practical for one family does not work at all for another family. Some need a large play area for children or a special place for dogs to romp. Others prefer to carve out small sections of grass.

When we moved to our home, we wanted a large grassy area for play. In our first redesign, we reduced the square footage of grassy space by half and shifted from bluegrass to the buffalo (*Buchloe dactyloides*) and blue grama (*Bouteloua gracilis*) mix. Some would balk at the delayed spring greening and early fall brown color of the xeric mix I have selected, but it suits the needs of my family. We planted shrubs and perennials on the berms that form the periphery of the grassy area. We enjoy having some grass for grandkids and dogs but realize that we can reduce that space in favor of other recreational options. I am ready to cut the grass section back by another third and add a shaded seating area surrounded by drought-resistant shrubs.

## *Step 4: Water efficiently*

Although we have lived in the same home for more than thirty years, we are still learning about the most efficient way to water our trees, grass, and gardens. We live in a rural neighborhood that has access to water rights. For many years, we watered our lawn and trees from the irrigation pond at the end of our street. Although it is a tremendous asset to own water rights in the West, we found that there were some drawbacks. It was difficult for us to justify watering a huge bluegrass lawn while local farmers were struggling with insufficient water. We wanted to learn about xeric gardening and apply some of that knowledge to the maintenance of our property. There was an upside to maintaining our water rights through paying annual dues but removing ourselves from the routine watering schedule. We could learn to water our xeric plantings efficiently and feel free to leave our home at times when we would otherwise have been occupied with watering.

One of our early irrigation strategies was watering the berms with overhead sprinklers. We learned we were using a system that led to evaporation and waste. The water was running down the driveway rather than into the soil to hydrate the trees. This year, we started with a free analysis of our existing irrigation system by experts from our city water department. We learned that since we last upgraded our sprinkler system ten years ago, the industry has continued to produce innovative ways to reduce waste and improve the efficiency of irrigation.

The benefits of having a water audit, which is free in most communities, include the following:

- Evaluation of how much water your current sprinkler system puts out
- Evaluation of soil type
- Recommendation for frequency of watering
- Determination of when to water
- Recommendation for amount of water for each section of the property

In addition, we learned some key tips to reducing waste while providing water. Watering between midnight and six o'clock in the morning is ideal because there is minimal loss due to evaporation. Setting the sprinkler to water each section of the garden by zone will allow plants with high water needs to receive more water and plants that are drought resistant to receive less. Another water-saving tip is to divide the watering cycle into two periods. Plants do best when they receive water for about ten minutes followed by another cycle of ten minutes.

The average homeowner uses twice the amount of water needed to water the lawn and gardens. Adding a few key strategies for water efficiently can put a big dent in water waste.

## *Step 5: Choose plants selected for your area*

There are numerous perennials, shrubs, and trees that thrive in Colorado. When I started gardening, I was easily bedazzled by the myriad colors and textures as I walked through local nurseries in pursuit of new plantings. I learned from trial and error and experienced more garden failures than I care to admit. Eventually, I started to read about plants that are native to Colorado, as well as plants that are recommended because of their ability to adapt to local weather and soil conditions. I used to be proud of my efforts to select plantings that were well suited to our environment and to the limited water resources. Now that I have a better understanding of native plants and their importance to the health of our world, I am concentrating on native species as I continue to modify our landscape.

We are ready to add some shade trees in our yard, and I am learning that one place to start is to make note of trees planted in the neighbors' yards. The experts at the CSU extension service recommend surveying the neighborhood to identify the species of trees that are planted and then intentionally planting something different. Planting a diversity of vegetation reduces the likelihood of disease that could wipe out large sections of landscape in the neighborhood. For example, I intend to plant a hackberry (*Celtis occidentalis*) tree, which is native and does not exist in our neighborhood.

When weeding the garden, the seasoned gardener can usually distinguish between a common weed and a perennial that was planted intentionally. But what can be done about the surprise appearance of perennials, shrubs, and even trees that weren't planted by the gardener? And perhaps more important, are the volunteer plants native or nonnative? I have talked with a number of gardeners who proudly point to a volunteer that has thrived and assumed a place of honor in the garden.

Surprises are fun and an important part of the gardening experience for me, but surprises can turn into nightmares. I will always remember my first garden volunteer, mint (*Mentha*). Why? Because I still have it! Anyone who has grown mint will know what I am talking about. It is a friend for life, so you had better develop a taste for it or be prepared to wage war indefinitely. Mint is found on every continent except Antarctica. Mint would be a happy plant if given lots of space to spread as a ground cover, but it can also be invasive. Managing mint is a great example of the challenges of having volunteers enter the garden stage.

Garden lights. That is what I name my sunflowers (*Helianthus annuus*) because they spread so much serendipitous joy to my garden. They volunteer every year, sometimes in predictable places and sometimes not. With a little plucking, thinning, and even transplanting, I manage to have a troop of them line my driveway like colorful soldiers, as if to salute visitors to our home. I also find them waving from surprising spots in shaded and sunny sections throughout the yard. Some people scoff and consider sunflowers a common weed, but I enjoy their volunteer efforts on behalf of my garden. Sunflowers are natives that have a colorful history. They were one of the first crops to grow in North America, and they have traveled to Europe and other parts of the world. They are part of my garden story.

When I first identified volunteers in my garden, I was thrilled and welcomed all comers. It didn't take long to realize that my attitude led to a troublesome free-for-all. Some of the newcomers became fierce interlopers that were in combat with planned plantings. It is incumbent on the gardener to identify volunteers that will become full-fledged members of the garden community and those that will need to be removed. I am reminded of a quote by Ralph Waldo Emerson: "What is a weed? A plant whose virtues have never been discovered."

Emerson's definition doesn't quite fit, though, when we consider the problem of noxious weeds. Noxious weeds are those plants that were introduced for whatever reason from another environment. They may have been perfectly suited in their original habitat because they were coexisting with predatory insects and plant pathogens. But when noxious plants were introduced, their companions did not travel with them. The proliferation of noxious weeds creates an imbalance that wreaks havoc on the environment. Noxious weeds and plants compete with indigenous vegetation and can drive the native plants out. Furthermore, the spread of noxious weeds can affect soil stability, wildlife habitat, and cropland. When we first moved to our property, I was delighted to see a little blooming vine that looked like a morning glory in our pasture. When I cheerfully showed my treasure to an old friend, she let the hammer fall pretty hard with the news that I had an invasive weed and not a pretty native flower. I learned that bindweed (*Convolvulus avernsis*), which comes from Europe and Asia, would be my foe for all time. When I spot that pretty flower in my pasture now, I am quick to remove it.

My husband and I established some of the trees on our property in 1984 when we built our home. The Colorado State Forest Service sells native trees and shrubs to assist conservation efforts in the state, provide edible landscape, stabilize soil, and enhance pollinators. In 1984, Russian olive (*Elaeagnus angustifolia*), along with a number of other species, was sold in bulk to people who owned more than one acre of property. In later years, this hardy shrub-like tree was placed on the list of invasive plants. It is difficult to get rid of this unwelcome member of my garden family, and the only comfort I find in keeping it is that small birds do like to seek refuge there.

At the same time, we also planted lilac (*Syringa*), which is native to the Balkan Peninsula; honeysuckle (*Lonicera*), widely distributed throughout North America; and chokecherry shrubs *(Prunus virginiana)* as borders around our yard. I continue to find them appearing in a host of new sites in my garden. Sometimes, the volunteers can stay, but when they threaten the lives of other species, they must go.

I have come to welcome volunteers that bring interest and harmony to the garden. But I am now ruthless in culling invaders that choke out planned plantings. At one time, I welcomed Virginia creeper (*Parthenocissus quinquefolia*) in my garden. But when it started to drape over my existing shrubs and trees to the point of burying them, it had to be yanked. Yet I have seen that same plant provide beauty and texture, hugging tall fences and the sides of buildings in our town. And Virginia creeper does have the benefit of being a native of North America.

Mayday trees (*Prunus padus commutata*) are present in numerous gardens and parks in our area. To my delight, several appeared in our yard a few years ago. This year, I have taken my garden shears to pluck unwanted volunteers, but I have left hardy specimens to grow and replace my diseased Aspen (*Populus tremuloides*). I am allowing the strongest members of the community to mature into a canopy of shade that will provide an abundance of shelter and food for the birds. This is not a decision that would work for everyone. I have learned that some gardeners consider Mayday trees to be invasive. Another downside is that they are not native; they originated in northern Europe and Asia.

Last year, I discovered a spectacular flower with multiple complex chambers in the large pink blossom growing happily in a semishaded section of one of my garden beds. After some research, I learned that it is a cleome spider flower (*Cleome spp.*). The lovely plant, which is considered a native, has returned in greater numbers this year, and I am pleased to welcome the flower to my garden. It is also called the Rocky Mountain bee plant—aptly named, because it is attractive to bees.

Another volunteer that has selected various areas of my garden to settle in is the milkweed (*Asclepias syriaca*). This is a particularly desirable addition to my garden family because it is one of the essential foods for the now-endangered monarch butterfly.

One year, I tossed a box of wildflower seeds in a section of my garden. They looked pretty good for one season, and then the wildflowers developed a plan of their own. The larkspur (*Consolida sp.*) was the solitary blooming plant that repeated year after year. It produced luxurious blooms of purple and pink in the late spring until this past year, when the bloom time was shorter and the dregs of the lingering stalks were unappealing. It was clearly time to remove the remains of the larkspur and instead plant a lower-maintenance shrub in that area.

The remainder of the wildflower seeds from that impulsive sprinkling of a single box danced on the summer winds to other sections of the garden and have appeared in the middle of other beds and smack in the center of one of my garden paths. I like the surprise of a Mexican hat bloom (*Ratibida columnifera*) appearing here and there, but they marched like an army across the width of my walking path so that no one could pass. That didn't work for me, so I had to use a firm hand to set some boundaries.

Siberian elm saplings (*Ulmus pumila*) readily volunteer in our area. Many gardeners consider them to be "junk trees" because they are relatively short lived and break in the fierce winds along the Front Range. But they do provide some shade and habitat for wildlife. I have allowed several to establish themselves as a barrier to noise and unsightly road traffic on the south side of our property. Now that I am learning more about the downside of the Siberian elm, we are planning to remove them entirely and replace them with trees that will thrive in our area.

## *Step 6: Mulch to reduce evaporation*

Mulch is the protective layer for the garden and a critical component to the success of xeric gardening. The addition of three to five inches of mulch over the soil helps hold moisture and reduce the volume of irrigation water needed. Another benefit is reduced time spent weeding. The mulch topping needs to be enhanced every two to three years to keep the protective covering at the recommended depth.

The most popular mulch for neighborhood landscapes is wood mulch. I made the decision to add it because I felt that it cooled the landscape and added a uniform look. While the addition of wood mulch is attractive, particularly in the northeastern part of the United States, which is heavily forested, some gardeners would argue that wood mulch does not belong in the western landscape design. A mixture for mulch recommended by Jim Tolstrup, the executive director of the High Plains Environmental Center, includes pea gravel mixed with three-quarters of an inch of tan river rock and squeegeed.

## *Step 7: Maintain the xeriscape*

I do many things for myself that fall under the heading of maintenance. I eat healthy food, see the dentist regularly, exercise daily, and keep a positive attitude. But for some reason, I turned a blind eye to the importance of certain maintenance activities for my trees, grass, and shrubs. Take aeration for example. I didn't understand the science behind pulling dense plugs out of the earth. Since I have learned about the benefits of aeration, I liken compacted soil to constipation. Nothing is moving down there! The plants were stunted in their ability to spread their roots and grow to their full capacity. Once I comprehended the limitations of the compacted soil beneath, I took action and hired a company to aerate our lawn. Living things require care. It's just that simple. I could almost see my trees breathe more freely last fall after their first aeration in many years.

Fall is a good time to fertilize our buffalo and blue grama grasses. It is also a good time to add compost to enrich the soil around perennials and shrubs. Our trees, shrubs, and lawn also need a final autumn drink before the dormancy of winter. Some of my friends are zealous about putting their gardens to bed in the autumn. In other words, they diligently cut back spent blooms and branches and add a layer of compost that can soak into the soil during the winter snows. There is a case, however, for leaving interesting plants and shrubs for winter interest.

During the winter months, I love to study my landscape and consider the need for pruning my young trees. The ideal time to prune is in the early spring before blooms appear. It is wise to be prudent with pruning, however. Gardeners are cautioned to avoid overpruning because birds need safe nesting places. Large shrubs along the north side of a property are ideal for birds and butterflies. I am delighted when it snows to quench the thirsty vegetation, and I mark my calendar to keep track of the moisture that nature is providing. When snow or rain are absent from the forecast, I follow a monthly watering of trees and shrubs during the winter months and before the irrigation system is operational.

JOURNAL PROMPTS

- Select one section of your garden that could be transformed into a xeric garden.
- Think of your garden as an extension of yourself and your values. Sketch a garden design that incorporates waterwise plantings.
- Review the seven steps of xeric gardening, and describe your approach to addressing each of those steps in your redesign.

# Nine

*The lovely flowers embarrass me.*
*They make me regret I am not a bee.*

—*EMILY DICKINSON*

One of the lessons I have learned as a garden-er is that I am not the master of my garden but rather a visitor who is fortunate enough to be a caretaker. The earth belongs not just to me but to the many forms of wildlife that thrive on the vegetation I plant. I like to think of my gardens as a haven for any wild creature that happens to wander there. In the thirty-plus years we have lived in our home, we have seen rabbits, foxes, squirrels, skunks, raccoons, a wild turkey, and numerous species of birds and other pollinators roam through our yard. We even had a deer wander off course and bound through the backyard on her way to safety.

The visitors we are especially interested in attracting are the pollinators. Pollinators are drawn to native species, many of which have radiant blooms. Native species are on the decline in the United States because of insect spray and a reduction in open space and biodiversity. There are numerous reasons to plant native species :

- Water conservation
- Resilience of the plant
- Won't become a noxious weed
- May be required by law, policy, or covenant
- Food and shelter for pollinators
- Reduce fragmentation of landscape
- Slow the loss of biodiversity

I was pretty proud of myself when I transformed from an occasional gardener in my cluttered life to an intentional gardener working with xeric principles. I thought if I continued to concentrate on waterwise principles, I would be an awesome gardener who was preserving my environment. I learned that I was not doing enough.

Now I recognize that the next step in my evolution as a gardener is to become a student of native plants and their partners. Planting with natives is considered bird-friendly landscaping because the birds are able to use food sources that are part of their food chain. In North America, 96 percent of birds feed insects to their young. Native insects coevolve with native plants and become the necessary food source for native birds to thrive.

The widespread tendency to landscape without considering the origin of the plant has led to depleted adequate food sources for native species. I used to think that a plant that adapted to our western environment would be a good-enough food source. Now I understand that a commitment to native landscaping is associated with an increase in quantity and diversity of birds.

The concept of "right plant, right place" mentioned earlier in this book is relevant for the adaptability of the plant, but it does not address the function of the plant. So, in addition to thinking about the beauty of the landscape and the application of water, it is important to evaluate the role of the plant in the lifecycle of pollinators who are visitors to the garden. When I plant with natives, I am preserving biodiversity in my environment. Birds are attracted to natives for food, shelter, a place to rest, and a place to nest.

Most plants that attract pollinators perform best when planted in large groupings, so the community of blooms is a clearly visible source of nourishment. Close spacing of plants provides a fullness and density that helps reduce the impact of the intense sun. This spring, I spotted a large, shrub-like plant tucked among the plantings in my aroma garden. After a bit of investigating, I learned that the plant is catmint (*Nepeta*). It joins the ranks of volunteers that I will keep because it is attracting a variety of pollinators.

I have a friend in town who claims she never sees hummingbirds, but I know to look for them from the middle of August, when they appear right on schedule. I have a habit now of looking at the showy orange hummingbird mint (*Agastache aurantiaca*) plants, where hummers are likely to appear in the morning and again in the late afternoon. The rush of their wings, the sheen of their green backs, and their focused intention of dipping into each flower cup for nourishment fascinate me.

Dragonflies are drawn to water, and although we don't have a pond, dragonflies do frequent our gardens during certain times in the summer when the humidity is high. I am mesmerized by their dance as they dart about the garden, serving as a cleanup squad as they go. Although I haven't seen this, I know they catch their prey midflight. They are able to eat hundreds of mosquitos a day.

I am embarrassed to report that it was just last year that I learned there is a difference between bumblebees and honeybees. Bumblebees are large and furry, while honeybees are smaller and thinner. The important thing for the gardener to know is that both are on the decline. I find both in abundance along with the hummingbird moth in my waterwise perennial beds.

There are more than nine hundred species of native bees. They live in the ground and need some bare soil for nesting. We have a variety of sections in our yard that provide habitat for the bees. It is a more difficult landscape option for the urban garden, but it's still doable.

To attract pollinators, it is crucial to refrain from using chemical sprays. Ladybugs and praying mantises work with me to curb the explosion of troublesome bugs, like aphids. Sevin, which was popular as an insect spray in the 1950s, is still in use but is dangerous to beneficial insects and to humans as well. According to the Audubon Society, approximately 40 percent of pollinating insects are threatened with extinction. This is particularly true of bees and butterflies. Pesticides and climate change are the primary culprits. Crops such as apples, broccoli, and almonds depend heavily on pollinators, and they could become scarce. That grim thought was enough for me to stop using pesticides.

Wasps—not one of my favorite winged creatures because of their sting—also contribute to the garden mix of helpful insects. They are pollinators, and they kill grubs, caterpillars, and weevils. As long as they are not in an area where they interfere with play or entertainment, I let them be.

When gardens are planted to attract birds, grateful gardeners are rewarded with the company of a variety of birds that are drawn to fruit-bearing shrubs, which double as welcome shelter. One local gardener who was featured on the Greeley Garden Tour was also a member of the Audubon Society, and he counted more than eighty species of birds that visited his yard. The same gardener was prompted to have his yard designated as a wildlife habitat. Another gardener featured on the Greeley Garden Tour deliberately planted species to attract butterflies and had her yard designated as a way station for monarch butterflies. The opportunities for attracting and enjoying pollinators are endless.

Judy Richter

**JOURNAL PROMPTS**

- Identify species in your garden that attract birds, bees, and butterflies.
- Who are the pollinators that visit your garden?
- What natives can be added to your garden to welcome pollinators?

# Ten

## POLISH THE GEMS

*Humankind has not woven the
web of life. We are but one thread
within it. Whatever we do to the
web, we do to ourselves. All things are
bound together. All things connect.*

—*CHIEF SEATTLE*

The gems that emerged as I uncovered my garden story presented themselves as I became ready to see and understand their significance. The garden gems provided important lessons for me, not just about gardening but about life itself. The garden has taught me that each of the gems continues to provide lessons when I take the time to recognize that I am a member of the living garden and not master of my garden community. I am the producer and director of my story, but my role frequently changes to that of observer or partner with the characters that are at the center of the story.

## *Roots*

I think of my own mortality more often now. I have lost some friends and seen health changes in others, and now that I am slowing down, I am acutely aware of the boundaries of my life. At the same time, I am refreshed and inspired by the timeless flow of the life of a garden. My garden will outlive me. That is not such a troubling thought. It is a happy paradox that I have been learning to be present in the garden but also to consider the needs of those who will follow me. The garden, when cared for properly, can transcend generations of people and wildlife that visit. This is, of course, true for the habitat around us as well. My home and garden are a microcosm of the abundant yet shrinking life on our planet. There are powerful stories of respect and the fight for the life and rights of the living world outside the garden walls. The gift of gardens extends to the life of the community.

A number of years ago, in a small New England town, a group of women circled ancient sycamore trees that had been planted along a road that once served as a trail. The trail had been used by the Lenape Nation and extended from Pennsylvania to the Jersey shore. The sycamore tree–lined road was later used by Washington's troops. The women's efforts were not part of a festival or ceremony. The small group of dedicated women was fighting to save the historic sycamore trees. The trees had been planted during the Revolutionary War to symbolize the strength of the thirteen original colonies. I was inspired by the story not so much because I grew up in the little town of Shrewsbury, New Jersey—where the elegant, dapple-trunked giants lined one of the main boulevards in town—but because of the deliberate action of the local women to preserve their ancient trees. They were just ordinary women, but their efforts were an unselfish statement about the importance of preserving historic trees. Eventually, the trees had to go because they were unstable. Too often, though, we let progress dictate the removal of trees and other vegetation that not only have historical and cultural importance but also support a host of wildlife.

It is humbling to realize that our ancestors embraced the value of trees with concern for our quality of life. The first Arbor Day in the United States was held in Nebraska in 1872, when one million trees were planted to celebrate the event. Arbor Day is now celebrated annually on the fourth Sunday in April. Because of the problem of deforestation, the celebration of Arbor Day is as important today as it was at its inception. Arbor Day is not a national holiday, and the day goes unnoticed by most. Yet our ancestors thought enough about their descendants to make a statement about the preservation of trees. The tree, through its abundance of gifts, is such a powerful symbol of strength, stability, nurturance, and hope.

Dedication of a tree to honor the loss of a loved one is a poignant demonstration of caring for one's roots while extending the gift of gardens to the community now and in the future. When my grandfather died, friends dedicated a cedar grove in a park that was being established in his town. My sister, Cathy, and I visited the park a few years ago and were inspired by the lush green forest that was once an untended piece of land. We realized that the garden park offered beauty and comfort for visitors of all ages.

I see myself as a placeholder in my garden, knowing that my children and grandchildren will have to pick up the rake and spade when I am ready to put down the tools. I like the notion that I am part of the chain of life that will continue long after I am gone. I can facilitate the continuity of the life-death cycle in the garden through my relationship with the next generations. I am a big fan of instilling in young children an interest in nature through the process of gardening.

I feel joy when I introduce my grandchildren to the many treasures found in a garden. It is never too early to start reading to kids to get them excited about the natural world they live in. There are so many books that tell captivating stories about gardens, bugs, and bees.

A great choice for a child of preschool or early grade school is *Miss Rumphius*, a story about an old woman who dreams of spreading joy to others by planting fields of lupine (*Lupinus hybrids*). A close family friend gave the book to our daughter when she was a toddler, and now our granddaughters enjoy the story. Sometime in early June, after reading the book as a bedtime selection to our little would-be gardeners, my husband promised that I (in the spirit of Miss Rumphius) would plant lupine for them! I embraced the idea, found some lupine at our local plant-and-produce store, and placed the little plants in an area that would get the water and attention they would need. The lupine is not only striking in appearance and color, but it attracts butterflies and hummingbirds.

Giving a kid his or her own little pot along with a bit of soil and some seeds is another great way to begin the lesson about the seed-to-life story. I attended an early spring birthday party for a three-year-old boy recently. The opportunity to pot a plant and dabble in the dirt was a favorite of the partygoers.

The garden produces gifts in obvious ways with showy flowers, tasty vegetables, diverse textures and colors in shrubs and ground cover, and cooling shade from well-placed trees. But there are some unexpected gifts as well in opportunities to share with others.

When my kids were in grade school, one of their favorite autumn activities was to visit the local fields, where migrant workers had completed their harvest. The local schools and churches were invited to come to the fields for gleaning. I had never participated in gleaning fields as a kid, and I was intrigued by the educational opportunities for the children as they participated in their treasure hunt of discarded and abandoned produce. One of the wise teachers introduced the story of *Stone Soup*, to enhance the experience. In the story, three soldiers help a French village learn the meaning of giving when they share a watery soup, flavored with a stone and a few simple vegetables, for nurturance. The lesson of abundance in sharing was not lost on the hungry kids.

When you begin the process of creating your garden story, spend time reflecting on your roots.

Perhaps as important, think of gifts in your garden that can be left behind for future inhabitants. What are some things you can do to instill a passion for gardening in your children and grandchildren?

## *Pause*

Before embarking on my garden story, I learned to walk through my garden at various times of day. When I visit my garden at different times of the day and in each season, I find clues about where I need to start over.

There is a rhythm to the colors, scents, sounds, and movements of the garden, and it resonates within me if I pay attention. A quote from Thoreau's *Walden* comes to me when I work in the garden: "An early morning walk is a blessing for the whole day." I know that when I allow myself a few extra minutes to start the morning with a walk around my yard, it sets my mood for the entire day.

I am present. It is easy to find gratitude in the simple pleasure of smelling lavender (*Lavandula angustifolia*) or watching the birds scratch the dirt for seeds from native shrubs. Early morning watering as I walk around my garden is one of my favorite rituals. As I water areas of my garden that need special attention, I think of my ancestors and their lives. They didn't have the luxury of sprinklers. They hand watered their vegetable gardens so they could nourish their families. I can't help but wonder if they had more focus as they started their day, intentionally caring for the life in their gardens. Now, as I water my little plants, I look at the new growth and consider which plants may need a new location, which ones need to be removed because of disease and overgrowth, and areas where new plants can be allowed to seed and take bloom. My life doesn't seem so significant when I think of myself as part of the larger world outside. Caring for my garden is much like caring for my family. It is one way to have a hand in caring for the world. The attention toward life in my garden brings new energy and life back to me and refreshes me for the day ahead.

The garden is a living opportunity to learn and to practice gratitude. It is all too common to go through life swept along by the currents of a demanding job while trying to care for a family.

Resentments creep in and take hold like insidious weeds in the garden. It becomes difficult to find the energy to complete the simplest of tasks. The cumulative toll of stress on the mind and body is evident in the volume of advertisements dedicated to antidepressants and stress-reducing products.

The garden offers an abundance for those who are open to learning. The garden can teach a lesson in gratitude with some simple steps. The first step is to be fully present. I pause. I take earbuds out of my ears and leave the cell phone in my house or car. When I pause, I am unencumbered by distractions and technological devices. I take the time to turn on all my senses. I tend to be predominantly a visual learner, but when I approach the garden, it is important that I am fully aware of all my senses as I take in my surroundings.

Let's say its spring, and the dandelions (*Taraxacum*) are in full bloom. It may be hard to look at a dandelion and feel gratitude. I have always thought of the dandelion as a weed that should be eliminated from my yard. But there is more to the story. When I tap into all my senses, my perspective shifts. The bright yellow attracts bees. The bees are endangered, and yet they are drawn to the simple dandelion that most would call a weed. I listen to the drone of the bee as it gathers nectar. I taste the leaf. Bitter! Some people actually make the greens into a salad and crush the flowers into wine. Have you shifted your perspective? Perhaps not, but you get the idea. Once you are open and alive to your garden and you practice gratitude, you are ready for a transformative garden experience.

You have the opportunity to create a space that embraces your values, dreams, and pleasures. Think about how you want to use your garden space. Some people want to develop a quiet place for reflection; for others, an active entertainment center or play area will take center stage. Are there pets to consider as you begin your design? Who are the cast of characters who will become part of your garden story?

I know it is tempting to buy plants on impulse. In this book, I have described some of the pitfalls of taking that approach. Like me, I suspect you will be so much more satisfied with the process of telling your story if you take the time to pause.

## *Start over*

Some gardeners take pride in landscaping their yards in a few years or less. I am in no rush. It has taken Walt and me ten years to add paths and a diversity of native trees, shrubs, and perennials; to try some projects that failed; and finally, to reach a point where we feel pretty good about the results. Not long ago, we noticed that one of the older sections of the yard is showing signs of age and decline. The cycle continues. The beauty and harsh reality of this living masterpiece are that it is never complete.

I have decided to refrain from the allure of the brilliant array of annuals. Yes, the abundant display of spectacular blossoms beckons me to purchase baskets and carve out sections of my garden beds to make room for their color and cheer. I am inspired by gardeners who have the talent and time to nurture native perennials and host an array of annuals as well. But I have learned the painful lesson over and over: the water needs of many annuals exceed the pleasure they produce for me and my family. Yet there are some exceptions. Zinnias (*Zinnia elegans*), which are part of the daisy family, produce lovely color all summer with minimal water and hassle once established. Many gardeners add them as a garden staple, and I understand why. Alyssum (*Lobularia maritima*) is also a robust annual that blooms from spring into late fall, and the tiny white flowers add a nice accent. This year, I tried a new approach with my pots. I planted perennials such as yellow stonecrop (*Sedum nuttallianum*) mixed with a colorful splash of petunias. Petunias (*Petunia atkinsiana*) are hardy, cheery annuals that pop color from pots amid my perennials, and they enhance the appearance of my garden beds.

One of the joys of gardening is the ability to engage wholeheartedly in the journey, knowing that it is an imperfect process. In my role of volunteer for the Greeley Garden Tour, I frequently ask avid gardeners if they would like to be on the tour. It is not uncommon for a gardener to shake his or her head adamantly, saying, "I'm not ready." For a number of years, I wondered about that and then solemnly went back to my own garden, bemoaning the areas that presented an overwhelming amount of work. Never mind being on a garden tour and sharing my garden with others, I couldn't even enjoy my own garden. When I looked at the areas of the garden that were problematic, I became discouraged and wondered if I would ever enjoy the results of the hard work. I can empathize with gardeners who are self-conscious and a bit embarrassed about showing their work. Once I started to relax about my gardening endeavors and realize that I am committed to a journey of discovery, I enjoyed the experience so much more. Now when I am in the garden, I am able to pause and take in one section at a time. When I approach my garden in this manner, I am able to appreciate the natural beauty in spite of the weeds that sometimes appear to be taunting me. I am able to tour my garden honestly and identify sections that need a jump start with perhaps some thinning or the addition of new members. I am also able to take a deep breath and recognize a section where I need to start over with a redesign. I have come to the conclusion that I have created a living space for me and my family that reflects who I am, and I am eager to share my journey with others.

## *Garden with intention*

Now I enter the garden with a plan, and when the plan isn't working, I look for clues about the interfering problem. Do you have a galloping garden like I did? Or is your garden just ho-hum and in need of a face-lift? Perhaps the garden is directing you to a new form of plant life that is more important for the garden story you are trying to create. When I approach the garden with intention and pay attention to the seasonal needs, I am able to follow and support the natural direction of the garden life cycle. My current plan is to evaluate my garden beds for the incorporation of natives.

## *Spring*

When I step into the garden in springtime, I inhale and smell the freshness of the earth. I feel restless and ready to get to the business of tilling the soil. Everything outside is new again. I admire the sparkle of the world in the faces of my early blooming flowers. The promise of life and transformation is evident in the community of shrubs, trees, and perennials, getting all gussied up for their performance in the brilliant spectacle ahead.

Spring is the time of year I am most likely to think of new plans for my garden. In the past, in my enthusiasm to watch something grow, I started seeds indoors. I have not had ideal results with that, but I know that early start-up activity works for many vegetable-gardening enthusiasts. I am more likely to spend my time outside trimming, pruning, pulling weeds, and generally cleaning up my garden. As I do that, I pay attention to areas where I can reorganize certain sections of my garden to increase diversity of texture, color, or form. I search for new locations for birdhouses while I engage in dividing, pruning, and planting.

Colorado had the wettest May on record in 2015. While many people were getting tired of the soggy weather, I donned my raincoat and garden boots and slogged through the rain and mud to transplant ground cover and to add compost to shrubs and perennials. I enjoy a cool, wet spring and can spend hours in the garden at this time of year and really enjoy the results.

Over time, I have learned that what works in one garden may not work in another, even in the same microclimate. For example, I know people who grow spectacular clematis, such as the elegant

*Clematis alpina*. I admit I love the radiant colors and lush blooms that drape over fences and mailbox posts. They don't do well in my yard because they require conditions that aren't a good match for my waterwise gardening perspective. There are three hundred varieties of this stately vine, but they all require cool, moist roots. There are other great blooms in springtime that do work in my yard.

We planted honeysuckle (*Lonicera periclymenum*) along one border of our property, and the fragrant scent of the downy yellow blooms is intoxicating as I walk along the periphery of my yard in the spring. Several years ago, I planted snowball viburnum (*Viburnum opulus*), aptly named for the large white clusters that do, indeed, look like snowballs. This hardy shrub grows along the back side of my berm on the south side of the property to add texture and color in the spring and entice birds to seek shelter all summer.

My favorite springtime perennials include yellow yarrow, white *(Salvia verticillata)* and blue (*Salvia ×sylvestris*) salvia, catmint (*Nepeta nepetella*), and red valerian (*Centranthus ruber*). With little attention other than deadheading, these plants will bloom all summer.

## Summer

I get up as early as I can to work in the garden. But as long as it is not too hot and I have my hat and sunscreen, I can be found most any time of day amid my blooms, pulling weeds, deadheading spent blossoms, and thinning overgrown perennials. By the Fourth of July, I am done with the projects I started with gusto in the spring. I wither along with my plants under the intense Colorado sun. I do enjoy studying the birds and insects that come to visit each season, and I make plans to expand perennials that attract native birds. We host our annual Greeley Garden Tour in the early summer, and I get ideas from each garden I visit that I would like to try in my own garden.

## Fall

This is my favorite time of the year to plant new shrubs and trees. The cost is reduced dramatically, I am not struggling with extreme weather to get the vegetation established, and the winter snows provide needed moisture. I am putting Mother Nature to work.

The crinkling of leaves crunching under my feet is my favorite sound in the fall garden. My primary garden activity in the fall is planting bulbs in preparation for the springtime parade after the cold silence of the sleeping garden.

Daffodils (*Narcissus pseudonarcissus*), tulips (*Tulipa gesneriana*), and crocuses (*Crocus vernus*) are wonderful ways to introduce my spring flower show. The first signs of little green shoots and then the pop of color that emerges from the crusty earth bring me so much joy that I remind myself to plant more each fall. Clusters of bright blooms from bulbs are placed where I can enjoy them as I come in and out of the house. In addition to the pleasure I get from the early harbingers of spring, I am nudged to engage in the more mundane garden chores that will ensure a healthy garden in the months ahead.

Some folks are pretty fastidious about remembering where they planted bulbs in previous years, marking the spots with Popsicle sticks or other markers. I don't do that. I consider myself lucky to remember to buy the bulbs. I plant them where it suits me, and if perchance I bump into an existing bulb while planting, I just move my spade a bit.

I came upon an article that addressed the merits of layering bulbs so that continuous bloom and color are present throughout the summer. This is an especially good idea for a gardener with a small amount of space.

I have friends who take pride in putting their gardens to bed for the winter. Not me. I don't like to create extra work and have learned that many shrubs and perennials do better with their spent blooms intact through the winter. Plus, I love the stark beauty of the winter garden and the contrast of russet brown grasses and velvet green pine trees laced with snow, all against the backdrop of a milky blue winter sky.

## *Winter*

Winter is when I first bonded with my garden during my stressful years as a nursing professor. I learned to pause and enjoy the landscape in the still of winter. I am continually refreshed by the opportunity to study the winter vegetation, learn about the wildlife that visit my garden, and dream about the garden that will beckon me in the spring.

Winter is an ideal time to identify space for a new birdhouse, shrub, or tree. The wonder that I experience in winter fills me with respect and awe.

## *Partner with pollinators*

When I consider my role as gardener, I realize how much I have grown and changed since I first picked up a spade and a packet of seeds. I have evolved from my early days of planting a seed, watching with pride as it grows into a cucumber plant, harvesting with delight my crop of bright-green goodness, and comparing the success of my efforts with the success of other weekend gardeners. I was the master of my little vegetable plot. But as I came to honor the power of the seasons, weather, and soil, I recognized that I was a helper or a facilitator rather than the master. The more I learned about the ways of the garden and the insects and birds that kept it thriving, the more I valued my role as partner with my garden community.

When a new neighbor moves into the neighborhood, I figure it is a good practice to welcome the newcomer and help him or her feel at home.

I enjoy bringing cookies or bread over to a new neighbor and introducing myself.

I also like to welcome the visitors to my garden. I aim to learn the names and needs of the trees, shrubs, and flowers that provide oxygen and joy for me, as well as habitat for wildlife. I don't remember all the names, but I like the process of learning about members of my garden family. I also try to identify a few of the birds and other pollinators that frequent my habitat. When I am acquainted with my outdoor life, I am more likely to develop practices of what I like to call environmental kindness.

Environmental kindness involves planting species that attract pollinators. Once the pollinators become regular visitors, they need a safe and nurturing environment. The gardener can help by limiting pesticides and by providing native plants for shelter and water.

## Summary

My garden story is a reflection of who I am: welcoming; cheerful; rambling; changing; surprising;

messy; and swirling with light and darkness, new blooms, and blossoms spent. My garden is not perfect, and neither am I. I have had Walt create paths through flowers and shrubs and some that flow to secret spaces for children, dogs, and fairies to explore. The imperfection of the art I have created leaves so many possibilities ahead. I have learned to savor the potential for crafting change with a spade, some determination, perseverance—and a plan! My garden is intended to be kind to the environment. And my garden story continues to evolve to include native vegetation that will attract pollinators.

Your garden may be a well-loved, old haven for family, friends, and wildlife. But perhaps you have a new space to create the garden of your dreams. You do not need a large space to begin your journey. The lessons you have learned and the stories I have told are yours now to change and to make your own. The time you spend in your garden is a gift to yourself that will keep on giving. So, get out there, get dirty, and have some fun.

## Journal Prompts

- What are key elements of your story that you want to embed in your garden project?
- Briefly describe your garden story.
- What changes need to be made to create or to change the plot for your story?

## Judy Richter Author Bio

Judy Richter is an avid gardener. After she retired from her career as a nursing professor at the University of Northern Colorado, she began spending more and more time in her garden.

Richter completed a certified gardener program at Colorado State University. She is experienced with many different aspects of gardening in the American West, including xeriscaping.

Richter is active in her community of Greeley, Colorado. She helps coordinate the Greeley Garden Tour and contributes to its companion booklet. Richter also has been published in the *Best of Greeley* magazine.

## *Sandy Baird Illustrator Bio*

Sandy has been drawing and watercolor painting for more than ten years since her retirement from nursing. What began as taking a watercolor workshop in Rocky Mountain National Park now involves painting with a passion. "My first love is to paint faces—people's, animals', and flowers'."

Sandy is the recipient of numerous awards for her painting from the Colorado Watercolor Society and the Greeley Art Association.